INTRODUCING PHILOSOPHY OF ART
IN EIGHT CASE STUDIES

Derek Matravers

ACUMEN

For Ed Winters and Vanessa Perry

First published in 2013 by Acumen

Acumen Publishing Limited

4 Saddler Street
Durham
DH1 3NP, UK

ISD, 70 Enterprise Drive
Bristol
CT 06010, USA

www.acumenpublishing.com

ISBN: 978-1-84465-536-6 (hardcover)
ISBN: 978-1-84465-537-3 (paperback)

British Library Cataloguing-in-Publication Data
A catalogue record for this book is available from the British Library.

Printed in the UK by the MPG Books Group.

CONTENTS

PREFACE AND ACKNOWLEDGEMENTS

I am grateful to Steven Gerrard at Acumen who first suggested this project, and has been a source of support throughout. The book has been much improved by suggestions from two anonymous readers, to whom I owe many thanks. There are several places where the argument was either improved or corrected outright. I am grateful to Gillian Rose for introducing me to the work of Nicolas Bourriard, to the late Charles Harrison for discussions of Rothko, to Jason Gaiger for discussions about the contemporary arts, and to Jon Phelan for discussions around Chapter 7. It will be evident how much I owe to the writings of Richard Wollheim and Malcolm Budd, the latter not always explicitly acknowledged and whose work is particularly evident in Chapter 2. Chapter 1 draws on an excellent forthcoming book by Dominic Lopes – *Beyond Art* – and I am grateful to him for sight of the manuscript. I also draw on an earlier book of his in Chapter 3. It is a pleasure to record my thanks to Jane Collins – and not only for providing me with the glorious room in which most of this was written. It is particularly important, given that my views on the matters that follow are not always widely shared, that I take responsibility for all errors, particularly any about which people have tried and failed to change my mind. Finally, it is a great pleasure to dedicate this book to Edward Winters and Vanessa Perry, in whose company I have spent many happy hours looking at pictures, listening to music and generally hanging out.

Derek Matravers

PLATES

INTRODUCTION

As philosophy is really just a matter of thinking deeply about things, and as art is one of the most fascinating things to think about, it is no surprise philosophers have things to say about art. In the past century or so, the list of things to think about in the arts seems to have multiplied. Largely unmodified objects such as urinals and beds appear to be art, as well as thoughts, lights that switch on and off, and walks in the countryside. This book aims to introduce eight debates in the philosophy of art through discussion of eight particular examples. Before launching into the first of these, I want to try to clarify what I am hoping to do in this book. First, I shall say something about the ambitions of the book. Second, I shall say something about the philosophical approach I shall be taking. Finally, I shall say something to distinguish the philosophy of art from other enquires that flourish in the same hedgerow.

What, then, of the book's scope? First, it does not attempt to cover all the arts. The focus will be on the visual arts rather than on music, or literature, or even architecture (if architecture is an art). There are complicated reasons for taking this narrow approach, some of which will be explored in Chapter 1. However, the basic reason is that the visual arts form some kind of unity; they have enough in common to give us something to discuss. The addition of music or literature makes it less likely that one will be able to come up with something that is true of everything under discussion. Second, I have not attempted to give an even-handed account of each of the philosophical theories currently on the table for each of the topics I shall discuss. Rather, I have been guided by the desire to reveal what I take to be fundamentally interesting about each topic: that is, to reveal what I think really is at issue and why it matters. As you will find, the faultlines of the problems are tracked by rival philosophical theories, so there will be plenty of those to

1

encounter. However, we will not encounter all of them. Those whose appetite is still undimmed can do their own research among the suggestions for further reading.

Our topic, the philosophy of art, is sometimes bracketed with another topic, aesthetics, to which it stands in a complicated relationship. The term "aesthetics" is derived from the Greek word *aisthanomai*, which means "I perceive". That is, "aesthetics" originally encompassed a whole range of issues to do with perception and consciousness. In the eighteenth century, the German philosopher Alexander Baumgarten narrowed the term and used it to refer to a particular kind of perception: the perception of beauty. This usage quickly took hold and survives to this day. It may appear obvious that the discussion of art will lead quickly to the discussion of beauty; after all, plausibly, being beautiful is the aim and purpose of works of art. Even if this were true, the discussion of beauty would have to cover much else besides art. There are plenty of things that are beautiful that are not art, such as roses, sunsets and other natural objects. Indeed, the character of the link between art and beauty has been the subject of much fraught discussion. We shall encounter this discussion throughout the book with questions as to what it is to be a work of art (which I consider in Chapter 1); questions about the link between art and expression (Chapter 3); issues to do with forgeries (Chapter 4); matters to do with interpretation (Chapter 5); and the link between art and knowledge, and art and morality (Chapters 7 and 8). In each case, the link between art and beauty is contentious; indeed, it is frequently denied that there is a link at all. As I do not want to stack the deck in favour of any particular view, I shall follow tradition and use "aesthetics" as the broad term for discussions of beauty, and "the philosophy of art" as the broad term to cover problems that arise from our thinking about the arts. By distinguishing the terms in this manner, I can use them without presupposing the nature of the relation between art and beauty.

Philosophers do not have a monopoly in thinking about these issues. Those who think about art constitute a broad church, encompassing philosophers of art, art historians, art theorists, art critics and artists themselves. Someone picking up this book might be seduced into thinking that the approach taken herein is the only possible approach. This is far from the truth as the different disciplines approach thinking about art in different ways. What follows is a sketchy map of the territory, so that I can locate this book somewhere on that map.

It may surprise those who are new to the subject that philosophy is a fairly Balkanized discipline. One tradition in philosophy stems from the eighteenth-century empiricists, and received a boost in the twentieth century from philosophers who were much influenced by logic and analysis such as Bertrand Russell and G. E. Moore. Philosophy in this tradition is referred to as "analytic" or "Anglo-American" philosophy (I shall use the latter label). English-speaking philosophy departments, if they do philosophy of art at all, tend to follow the Anglo-American approach and this book is in the Anglo-American tradition. The label for philosophy that is done in the other tradition is "continental philosophy". This embraces traditions in German, French and other philosophies that may not have much in common with each other. As I write, it is the continental tradition that tends to dominate outside philosophy departments, particularly in the art schools. The nature of the distinction between the Anglo-American tradition and the continental tradition is much disputed, so any attempt to characterize it will be tendentious. I shall, rather pusillanimously, remain silent on the issue.

Although the book does follow the Anglo-American tradition, it is unusual in its detailed discussion of particular examples. The fact that philosophy is standardly pitched at a high level of abstraction, focusing on general truths, militates against focusing too much on examples. If one wants to say something abstract and general about all cars, then it will not do to focus too much on one particular car (one might end up saying something that is only true of *that* car). However, a detailed discussion of examples can perform a number of useful functions. First, it keeps the discussion grounded in problems that arise in the case of real works of art, which stops us straying too far into the philosophy dreamworld. Second, it can keep us honest in the sense of providing us with a touchstone against which to check some of the claims we are making. In 1914 Clive Bell wrote, in his book, *Art*, the following much ridiculed passage: "The starting-point for all systems of aesthetics must be the personal experience of a peculiar emotion. The objects that provoke this emotion we call works of art. All sensitive people agree that there is a peculiar emotion provoked by works of art" (Bell 1928: 6).

What provoked readers of this passage was the appeal to "all sensitive people". This gave the impression that Bell was talking to himself and his coterie of aesthetes who were revelling in this "peculiar emotion", and those of us who are a stranger to it are by definition not sensitive. There is something to this criticism of Bell; at least, he does little to dispel it in other parts of his book. On the other hand, there is also something to Bell's view. Art (at least, most art) is bound up with experience; we are familiar with the pleasure (or with other sorts of value) that works of art can give us (we shall explore more of this in Chapter 2). Familiarity, however, is not understanding. One role for philosophy is to throw what light it can on the kinds of experiences these are: to make us conscious of, and reflective about, our everyday experiences. This way of putting the matter brings out the point at issue; we need to be familiar with these experiences in order to know whether what the philosopher is claiming makes sense. We will not know if someone has really explained what it is to access the value of art through experience if we are totally unfamiliar with that experience. It might not be, as Bell claims, "the starting point for all systems of aesthetics", but unless we know what engaging with art is like, we will not know whether what philosophers say about engaging with art is right. The second reason to engage with particular artworks, then, is to remind ourselves of what it is we are seeking to explain.

So much for the ambitions of this book and the approach it takes; what of the similarities and differences between philosophy and the cognate disciplines that also enquire into the arts? As none of these disciplines is particularly well defined, the similarities and differences will not be very specific. However, there does seem to be at least one characteristic area of difference that it might be worth saying a little about now as it will return several times in the chapters to come: the attitude to history or, more generally, the passing of time.

I shall illustrate this by drawing an analogy between producing a work of art and contributing to a conversation. What is it to understand a contribution to a conversation? One set of features of the contribution we might examine fall under the label "contextual". By examining what was said immediately before the contribution we can explain why the contribution had the form it did. We can also judge the value of the contribution's effect on the conversation. Was it an interesting response to what had just been said? Did it serve to take the conversation on in an interesting direction? Another set of features we might understand fall under the label "acontextual". These features are independent of the effect on the conversation. Instead, they are features the contribution has independent of the particular time and place at which it was made. These might be the internal features of the contribution (the relation between the form of the sentence and its content), the balance of the language that makes up the contribution, or such matters as the use of linguistic tropes or imagery. Acontextual features are likely to play a greater part in understanding a contribution to a conversation if that conversation is not going anywhere: that is, if people are simply talking, without really worrying about responding to each other or trying to argue to a point.

The question to consider is whether, when it comes to works of art, we should be contextualist or acontextualist. (The question is complicated by the fact that there are two sorts of contextualist, but I shall deal with that presently.) That is, in discussing a work of art, should we look at it in relation to the society in which it was produced and the ideas of its time, or should we extract it from that context and look at it (for want of a better way of putting it) "on its own terms". Art historians tend to be contextualist; indeed, that is what makes them art *historians*. Philosophers also recognize the need for contextual understanding. The questions "What is art?", "What is the value of art?" and "What does this work of art mean?" all require, at least to an extent, contextual understanding (I shall argue this in Chapters 1, 2 and 5, respectively). The focus of interest of philosophy, however, is not on contextual features. It is in the nature of philosophy to stand back from particular enquiries and ask general questions. This is not to say that philosophy limits itself to acontextual features; rather, it is one task of philosophy to ask acontextual questions about contextual features. To revert to the analogy, it asks questions such as: "What *is* a contribution to a conversation?", "What would make a contribution to a conversation interesting?" and "What is it for a conversation to go in an interesting direction?" These questions are general and thus not about particular contributions made in particular contexts. That is, they are not contextual or historical questions; rather, they ask acontextual questions about contextual features. They attempt to throw light on certain important concepts, including the concept of "a contribution" and the concept of "the interesting".

Answering these conceptual questions (i.e. acontextual questions about contextual features) may require that we bring in acontextual features. Among what makes a contribution to a conversation interesting might be a feature (the relation between the form of the sentence and its content, for example) that would make *any* contribution to a conversation, considered independently of the context of its utterance, interesting. Hence, while art historians (at least, when operating as historians) tend to focus on the contextual features of a work, philosophers of art tend to focus on acontextual questions about contextual features, and also on acontextual features.

The analogy is fairly rough but, I think, helpful. I said above that there were two sorts of contextualist. I have characterized the historian as someone who, in attempting to understand a contribution to a conversation, focuses on its contextual features. Historical enquiry need not be limited to contributions made at any particular time; all that is required is that when it picks on a contribution to study, it studies the contextual features of that contribution. However, there is another sort of contextualist: someone whose focus is on contributions to the *current* conversation. That is, someone who is interested in where the conversation is *now*, and what the best contribution would be *at the moment.* I shall call the art-world analogue of such a person – rather stipulatively – an art theorist. The boundary between the art theorist and the artist is not fixed; both are involved in thinking about the nature of contemporary art practice.

As I have described it, the roles of the philosopher, the art historian and the art theorist need not conflict (furthermore, a single individual can occupy more than one role). In a celebrated quotation, the American abstract painter Barnett Newman said, "Aesthetics is to artists what ornithology is to birds". Although Newman might have intended his comment to be dismissive, I think his characterization is accurate and informative. Thinking theoretically about art is not practising art any more than observing birds is practising being a bird. However, a focus on understanding contemporary art practice has led some art theorists to be sceptical of acontextual approaches, and hence sceptical about the value of philosophical approaches to art (whether that approach is one of being acontextualist about contextual features or simply being acontextualist). My view is that this is one of the reasons why philosophy these days has so little impact in art schools. I shall conclude this introduction by examining one particularly influential art theorist who is sceptical of the kind of philosophy I have been describing, in order to see if there is anything that should prompt us to rethink our approach.

In a recent book that has been very influential in the contemporary teaching of art, Nicolas Bourriaud has laid down a challenge:

> Where do the misunderstandings surrounding 1990s art come from, if not a theoretical discourse complete with shortcomings? An overwhelming majority of critics and philosophers are reluctant to come to grips with contemporary practices. So these remain essentially unreadable, as their originality and their relevance cannot be perceived by analysing them on the basis of problems either solved or unresolved by previous generations. (Bourriaud 2002: 7)

Bourriaud's claim is that the theoretical discourse surrounding the arts is inadequate to understand "contemporary practices". Bourriaud calls the kind of art he favours "relational aesthetics" or "participatory art". It is exemplified in the following work by an artist he discusses in some detail: Rirkrit Tiravanija.

> A metal gondola encloses a gas ring that is lit, keeping a large bowl of water on the boil. Camping gear is scattered around the gondola in no

particular order. Stacked against the wall are cardboard boxes, most of them open, containing dehydrated Chinese soups which visitors are free to add the boiling water to and eat. *(Ibid.: 25)*

That is, what Tiravanija's "work of art" consists of is food being made available and shared. Bourriaud has a particular view about where art (or at least art that matters) is now. Instead of artists being based in studios and producing objects, artists are part of "the socio-economic arena" and focus on "producing relationships with the world" *(ibid.: 68)*. Art has moved on. These days, an artist cooks a meal or runs a cafe rather than produce an object. Bourriaud puts the point as follows: "the artist sets his sights more and more clearly on the relations that his work will create among his public, and on the invention of models of sociability" *(ibid.: 28)*. Although (I assume) Bourriaud does not think there is anything wrong in the approach art history and philosophy take to understanding *past* art, he thinks their approach is unsuited to understanding *contemporary* art (or at least the art of the 1990s). Here is what he writes in his Glossary entry for the word "art":

1. General term describing a set of objects presented as part of a narrative known as *art history*. The narrative draws up the critical genealogy and discusses the issues raised by these objects, by way of three sub-sets: *painting, sculpture, architecture*.
2. Nowadays, the word "art" seems to be no more than a semantic leftover of this narrative, whose more accurate definition would read as follows: Art is an activity consisting in producing relationships with the world with the help of signs, forms, actions and objects.

(Ibid.: 107)

In his first paragraph Bourriaud reverses what one might think of as the natural order of explanation. Instead of defining "art history" in terms of what it is a history of – that is, art – he defines "art'" in terms of "art history". Works of art are those objects that are connected together by the narrative of art history (we shall see a similar approach to the definition of "art" in Chapter 1). Let us put that aside as it is the second paragraph that is relevant to us here. Bourriaud implies that the narrative of art history has come to an end, and has left the word "art" as a "semantic leftover". Putting the point in my terms, Bourriaud's claim is that the acontextual questions philosophy has asked do not apply to contemporary art practice. If this is right then this book, considered as a *general* introduction to the philosophy of art, is a failure. The examples I have chosen are all more-or-less traditional works (although, of course, what counts as "traditional" depends on that to which the works are being compared). Philosophy looks very much to be stuck in the past century or, given its obsession with beauty, possibly even stuck in the eighteenth century.

Is Bourriaud right? There are two reasons for thinking that he is not. First, there is some reason to be sceptical of the strong historicist line that characterizes Bourriaud's discussion of the development of art. Bourriaud's view is, to some extent, encouraged by the analogy I have used above: thinking of the history of art as analogous to the development of a conversation. He has focused on particular contemporary contributions to the arts (i.e. those who aim to invent "models of sociability") and come up with a theory that explains what the artists making those contributions are doing. He has then taken his theory to be the right approach (or at least a noteworthy approach) to contemporary art in general. Why, however, select *them*? Their work is only one tiny part of the enormous wealth of contemporary art practice. Bourriaud would need to defend his approach by claiming that the works he discusses are particularly noteworthy; they are where *the* cutting edge of the development of art is currently found. However, unless one is immensely selective about what one takes to be noteworthy in contemporary art practice, it is difficult to see how this could be justified.

Bourriaud is aware of this problem and tries to meet it by arguing that the artists in which he is interested have a good answer to a problem that affects us all (Bourriaud 2002: 16). It is a familiar complaint in Marx that capitalism reduces all human relations to money-relations and gradually deprives the sphere of human relations of meaning. Bourriaud claims that contemporary art practice is striving to comment on this fact and, in doing so, has put itself beyond the reach of the kind of theorizing that was characteristic of the philosophy of art in the past. Let us, for the sake of argument, grant that Marx's complaint about capitalism is correct. We should also grant, as it is true, that art should concern itself with the important problems of our time. However, there is a large stretch between this and the claim that the philosophy of art is redundant when it comes to understanding contemporary art, which is my second reason for disputing Bourriaud's conclusion. Many disciplines (including philosophy, politics and sociology) concern themselves with important problems of our time and comment on Marx's problem. We can ask of any such comment whether or not it is helpful and illuminating. That is not the question we ask about a work of art, however. Here the question is more like: *within the scope of being a work of art*, is anything interesting being said about Marx's claim? However, the first bit of that question introduces all kinds of issues and constraints that Bourriaud does not fully acknowledge.

The problem for Bourriaud is implicit in his Glossary definition above. He claims both that "art" is a "semantic leftover", and that he wants to give it a "more accurate" definition. These do not sit happily together. The first claim is that the narrative of art history has come to an end, and there has been a semantic rupture such that "art" either means nothing or does not mean what it meant previously. The second claim implies continuity: that the term "art" still has currency and that all it needs is a more accurate definition. The danger for Bourriaud is in a looming dilemma. Either artists such as Tiravanija represent a radical break from the past or they do not. Let us consider the first horn of the dilemma: that they represent a radical break. This immediately raises the question as to why – to use the example introduced above – what is being produced is art rather than a (fairly awful) dinner party. If it is the function of artists to "invent models of sociability" then why is that not simply inventing models of sociability? Why would we even think of it as falling within the domain of art? Let us then try the second horn of the dilemma. If Tiravanija does not represent a radical break with the past then the question of why what he is doing is art is easily answered: it is continuous with the work of artists in the past. However, if what Tiravanija is producing is art then we have what looks to be a standard philosophical question: what makes it art, as opposed to some other thing?

There is still work for philosophy to do, albeit a historically sensitive philosophy. We should not, however, leave Bourriaud's radical views behind altogether. There is, as we shall see, a strain of pessimism within philosophy that holds that the current art world is so radically heterogeneous that it defies the kind of abstract generalizing typical of philosophy. I said above that we can make sense of the questions "What is art?" and "What is the value of art?" Whether these questions are themselves as straightforward as I have suggested is one of the questions posed in Chapter 1, to which I now turn.

1. WHAT IS ART?

Yves Klein's *Anthropometries*

On a clear night in March [1960] at ten pm sharp a crowd of one hundred people, all dressed in black tie attire, came to the Galerie International d'Art Contemporain in Paris. The event was the first conceptual piece to be shown at this gallery by their new artist Mr. Yves Klein. The gallery was one of the finest in Paris.

Mr. Klein in a black dinner jacket proceeded to conduct a ten piece orchestra in his personal composition of The Monotone Symphony, which he had written in 1949. This symphony consisted of one note.

Three models appeared, all with very beautiful naked bodies. They were then conducted as was the full orchestra by Mr. Klein. The music began. The models then rolled themselves in the blue paint that had been placed on giant pieces of artist paper – the paper had been carefully placed on one side of the gallery's wall and floor area – opposite the full orchestra. Everything was composed so breathtakingly beautifully. The spectacle was surely a metaphysical and spiritual event for all. This went on for twenty minutes. When the symphony stopped it was followed by a strict twenty minutes of silence, in which everyone in the room willingly froze themselves in their own private meditation space.

At the end of Yves' piece everyone in the audience was fully aware they had been in the presence of a genius at work, the piece was a huge success! Mr. Klein triumphed. It would be his greatest moment in art history, a total success.

(Lewis 1960)

Above is a contemporary description of an event organized by the French artist Yves Klein (1928–62). After rolling around in the paint, the models pressed themselves against the paper, forming an impression of their bodies. Klein dubbed such works *Anthropometries* ("Anthropometry" is the measurement of the human body with a view to determining characteristics such as the average dimensions and so on). Let us leave aside for the moment the question of what exactly the purported work of art is – is it the event itself or the resulting impressions of the models' bodies? – and ask ourselves the obvious question. Rolling beautiful naked bodies in paint and pushing them against giant pieces of paper while dressed in a dinner jacket sounds marvellously good fun, but is it art? Indeed, we can polarize the debate. Let us call those who think that this is not art but some kind of elaborate con that has now been going on for far too long "traditionalists", and those who think that Klein's work is art, "radicals".

If two people are faced with an object and one says it is not a camel and the other says it is a camel, they will be able to sort out their disagreement only if they both know what a camel is. Similarly, we will be able to sort out the disagreement between traditionalists and radicals only if we are clear as to the nature of the disagreement. In short, before we can make any progress on whether Klein's work is art we need to work out what it is for an object to be a work of art. The traditionalist thinks he or she knows what art is, and is pretty sure Klein's work *is not* art. The radical also thinks he or she knows what art is, and is pretty sure Klein's work *is* art. It looks as if we have an unproductive stand-off.

The Cambridge philosopher Frank Ramsey held that it is a good rule of thumb that, in the face of apparently intractable arguments, one should look to see if there is something on which both sides agree that might be false. The obvious thing on which both sides agree in our case is that there is only one clear definition of "art". Where they differ is that each thinks they have the correct definition and the other side does not. The traditionalist thinks that art is something like this: it takes skill to produce, it has to be worthwhile to experience, it has to be beautiful, and (possibly) it has to look like something. The radical will probably grant that what the traditionalist thinks is art is in fact art, but argue for a much broader definition: that something can be art if it challenges us, if it extends the boundaries of art or, at the limit, if someone who is an artist says that it is art. It is no wonder they do not agree. It would be as if one side of the argument said that a camel was a beast of burden that had humps for storing water and the other side said that while that was true, being a camel also encompassed anything that had wheels.

Who, then, is right – the traditionalist or the radical? How are we going to answer this question? One thing is clear: neither side is simply allowed to make definitions up. The person who believes that anything that has wheels is a camel is wrong. Such a definition would do nothing to clarify our thoughts about camels. So how do we find out what the word "art" means? Where do we get our definition of "art" from? Perhaps surprisingly, when we start to probe the answer to this question we find that the presupposition on which the traditionalist and the radical agree is indeed suspect: it is not obvious that there is only one clear definition of "art". To see this, we need to take a good look at both definitions, in particular, the circumstances in which the traditionalist's and the radical's concepts of art arose.

The traditionalist's concept of art is basically the concept of "fine art", which encompasses music, poetry, painting, sculpture and dance. Some other art forms, particularly architecture, are somewhere on the margins and literature (as I mentioned in the Introduction) is best left to one side. In the 1950s, the formidable art historian Paul Kristeller argued that the concept of the fine arts had not always been with us but in fact is a fairly recent innovation. Hence, it is not like concepts such as "person" and "object", which have, I suppose, been around since we could first think, and more like concepts such as "death certificate" and "human resources development manager", which turned up when the time was right for them to turn up, and will fade away if we no longer need them. Kristeller surveyed a vast amount of writing on the arts from the past and came up with some surprising conclusions. The ancients, he says, "left no systems or elaborate concepts of an aesthetic nature, but merely a number of scattered notions and suggestions" (Kristeller 1951: 506). In medieval times, "the fine arts are not grouped together or singled out … but scattered among various sciences, crafts, and other human activities of a quite disparate nature" (*ibid.*: 509). It is only in the eighteenth century (1746, to be precise) that a French philosopher, Charles Batteaux, finally gave us the grouping that the traditionalist favours today (Kristeller 1952: 20). He listed music, poetry, painting, sculpture and dance together, claiming that they all evoked pleasure and also all imitated beautiful nature.

As a definition this needs some work. Let us start with the notion of "evoking pleasure". This is undoubtedly part of the rewards of art: it is enjoyable to look at paintings or listen to music. "Pleasure" and "enjoyment" are words that cover a wide variety of cases, however. Activities such as sitting in the sun or chewing a toffee give us pleasure, but is that the same kind of pleasure that we get from a work of art? It might be the same for some art, but if all we took from art was the same as that which we took from sitting in the sun or sucking toffees then it would be difficult to see why we think art more valuable than sitting in the sun or sucking toffees. I am not going to argue that art is more valuable here; I shall say some more about that matter in the next chapter. What I want to do here is allow for the possibility that some works of art provoke states of mind that go beyond these simple pleasures. The term that is generally used here to describe those states of mind is "the aesthetic experience".

What exactly counts as an aesthetic experience has been much discussed without that discussion resulting in any very precise conclusion. According to Baumgarten, it is the experience of beauty. It would not be very helpful for us to take this as a definition because, when we ask what "beauty" is, the obvious answer is that it is whatever it is that provokes the aesthetic experience; the two terms are defined in terms of each other. However, we are not left totally without resources for a definition. We can take the aesthetic experience to be a particularly valuable form of pleasure: value that does not only involve our feelings but also involves our minds. Looking at art (at least, looking at worthwhile art) is not a simple pleasure like sitting in the sun or sucking a toffee, but is an experience that involves thinking, feeling free from the humdrum concerns of everyday existence, and other such worthwhile satisfactions (Beardsley 1982).

The second clause of the definition concerns "imitating beautiful nature". This might seem unduly restrictive. After all, "imitating beautiful nature" does not apply across the disciplines Batteaux listed. There is very little music that imitates nature, and it often sounds a bit silly when it tries (on the other hand, an extreme traditionalist might want painting to imitate nature in the sense that paintings ought to look like what they are paintings of). However, we weaken the definition significantly if we drop the second clause, for doing so would leave us unable to distinguish between art and nature. The first clause of our purported definition would include many natural objects because there are flowers, birds and landscapes that provoke the aesthetic experience. These are excluded from the definition by the second clause because these things do not *imitate* beautiful nature: they *are* beautiful nature. The most plausible way out of these problems is to find another way of excluding nature. We could say that a work of art was something that was made with the *intention* that it should provide an aesthetic experience (this is similar to the definition offered in Beardsley 2004). This would exclude nature because nature was not made by anyone and so not intended to be a certain way by anyone.

Drawing all this together, we get the thought that the concept of art that we inherit from the eighteenth century, which is the traditionalist's concept of art, is that works of art are those objects which are made with the intention that they provide an aesthetic experience. Given this definition, the traditionalist will reject much of the art of the past one hundred or so years because much of this work was clearly *not* made with the intention of providing an aesthetic experience. Included among these will be some of the controversial works of modern art: the urinal signed and exhibited by Marcel Duchamp as *Fountain* (1917); Carl Andre's *Equivalent VIII* (1966; a number of fire bricks laid out horizontally on the floor); and contemporary examples such as Jake and Dinos Chapman's mutilated mannequins of children. These do not fall under the traditionalist's definition and therefore, according to the traditionalist, are not art. That is, the traditionalist can happily keep the definition narrow; if it excludes some things that other people call "art", then so much the worse for those things and those people.

Although narrow in some respects, the traditionalist's definition looks too wide in others. There are plenty of things that appear to be intended to provide an aesthetic experience that nobody thinks are art. Indeed, most things that are made for human beings to use are designed to provide some kind of aesthetic experience, from Dualit toasters to Ducati motorbikes. If this is right, then all products of good design would seem to be art by the traditionalist's definition. How could the traditionalist reply to this? One option would be to bite the bullet; to allow that all products of good design are art. After all, it is easy to imagine our admiring a beautiful motorbike and saying "that is a work of art". This, however, seems a desperate measure. We do say of motorbikes that they are works of art, but we also say this of cakes and pantomime costumes. In such cases we do not mean that these things are *literally* works of art; rather, we are using the word metaphorically or as hyperbolic praise (as we might call a favourite niece "a princess" or a worthy neighbour "a giant among men"). If the traditionalist allowed in all products of good design their definition would be very wide indeed. A second option would be to change the definition so that works of art are objects where the *primary* intention is to provoke an aesthetic experience. The primary intention behind toasters is to toast, and that behind motorbikes is to get from one place to another. Hence, by this revised definition, they would not count as art. This might help exclude some things but not others. The *appearance* of a toaster is not intended to toast and various bits of a motorbike have little or no engineering function. Would those things be art? Also, this revision looks in danger of making the definition too narrow: architecture would cease to be an art as the primary intention behind buildings is not that they provoke an aesthetic experience. A third option would be to refine the notion of the aesthetic experience to capture only those states of mind provoked by what we pre-theoretically think of as art, and not what we pre-theoretically think of as design. That seems even more desperate; is the state of mind of looking at a beautiful work a different *kind* of state of mind from that of looking at a beautiful piece of design?

Let us put aside until later this problem for the traditionalist's theory. It is easy to see that anyone who has this definition is going to be suspicious of Yves Klein's work. It seems like a joke: in what way does Klein's work belong to the category that includes such pieces as Mozart's *Requiem*, Rembrandt's *The Night Watch* and Michelangelo's *David*? Listening to a piece of music that is simply a single note for twenty minutes does not provide an aesthetic experience; it simply exasperates. Furthermore, what aesthetic reward is to be taken from seeing the impression of a paint-smeared human body on paper, which is, after all, only a larger scale version of finger-painting?

The key question, which throws light on the dispute between traditionalist and radical, is that if the concept of art can be "invented" once, why can't it be "invented" twice? It was not an accident that the traditionalist concept of art appeared when it did; that great upheaval in human thought, the Enlightenment, was in full swing. It was as if people had suddenly rediscovered leisure and intellectual enquiry; the arts and philosophy were flourishing, and the first novels (by Defoe and Richardson) had all been published within thirty years of Batteaux' grouping. The prevailing cultural mood was ripe for just such conceptual innovation. Simplifying somewhat, there was leisure time to be had, so there was space for the notion of something to be enjoyed simply for the sake of enjoying it. The key point, and the clue as to why we might have more than one concept of art, is that the Enlightenment has not been the only great upheaval in human thought. There has been another more recently, and it goes under the name "modernism".

In the visual arts, modernism is usually taken to start around the 1860s with the work of Manet. There is some dispute about when it ends, but the majority view is sometime in the 1960s. Let us begin with a plausible story. The end of the nineteenth century and beginning of the twentieth saw huge social and political change: there was mass industrialization, the rise of a self-conscious working class, wars in Europe, the shattering of social mores and much else besides. Virginia Woolf remarked (with some exaggeration) that "on or about December 1910 human character changed" (Woolf 1924). Art, or at least the visual arts, were under pressure from two sides. First, as had happened in the eighteenth century, art was not immune from the rest of society; it needed to respond to events. Second, there was a more particular concern. According to Batteaux, as we have seen, part of what makes the arts

arts is that they "imitate beautiful nature": one of the functions of paintings is to capture the way the world looks. *The Night Watch* captured the appearance of the night watch. The more particular concern was that this function was now being taken over by seemingly more efficient and accurate technologies. The first mass-produced camera – the Kodak Brownie – was marketed in 1900, and the Lumière brothers started projecting films in 1895. Art, or at least visual art, had lost the role Batteaux had found for it.

According to at least one form of modernism, this crisis of confidence in the arts brought with it its own solution. Deprived of the role of capturing the way the world looked, art was forced to look in on itself: to conduct a thorough investigation of its own nature. In the words of the distinguished modernist theorist Clement Greenberg, "The essence of Modernism lies, as I see it, in the use of the characteristic methods of a discipline to criticize the discipline itself, not in order to subvert it but in order to entrench it more firmly in its area of competence" (Greenberg 1992: 308). Before the end of the nineteenth century, art had explored its nature as something that captured appearances and could be enjoyed for its own sake. However, now the search needed to broaden; the content of art, what individual works of art were about, was the nature of art itself. In 1748, Batteaux had given us the traditionalist concept of art; in or around 1914, artists such as Marcel Duchamp gave us a different concept of art – the modernist concept of art.

What is this concept? Batteaux, as we have seen, gave us a two-pronged definition: art could be enjoyed for its own sake and imitated beautiful nature. What is the modernist definition? Let us jump forwards fifty years and consider a famous work of art that became a famous philosophical example: Andy Warhol's *Brillo Boxes* (1964). A Brillo box (that is, the "mere real thing" not the work of art) is a plywood box with a design on it that was used to store and transport Brillo Pads (a household cleaning product). Warhol made some plywood boxes to the exact size and screenprinted the designs on the side. What he produced were boxes that were visually indistinguishable from the mere real thing.

When the philosopher Arthur Danto saw these exhibited at the Stable Gallery in New York he had a revelation. Here were objects that were art that were visually indiscernible from objects that were not art. This prompted him to ask the question: what is it for the one set of objects to be art and the other set of objects not to be art? If we had asked the question of a traditional work of art, the answer would have been in terms of the object's appearance: *The Night Watch* not only captures the appearance of the night watch but also does it in a way that provokes the aesthetic experience – something that is valuable for its own sake. However, in this case it cannot be the way Warhol's *Brillo Boxes* look that makes them art because supermarket Brillo boxes look exactly the same. Instead, Danto argued, what it is for them to be art requires something that was not perceptual: "To see something as art requires something the eye cannot descry – an atmosphere of artistic theory, a knowledge of the history of art: an artworld" (Danto 1995: 209).

In short, according to Danto the difference between the *Brillo Boxes* that are art and the Brillo boxes that are mere real things is that the former are *about* something: art. Remembering that the role of art is self-inspection, the *Brillo Boxes* are (to put the point briefly and inadequately) about the fact that art can be deadpan and mass produced rather than unique and deeply expressive. The Brillo boxes, in contrast, are not about anything at all: they are merely boxes for storing and transporting household products. Danto is giving us an account of the content of a work of art: that is, what we need to understand if we are to understand a work of art. Danto would agree that if one was faced with the *Brillo Boxes* and one did not know anything about "the atmosphere of artistic theory [and] a knowledge of the history of art", one would not understand them. It would be as if one were in some foreign country and faced with an inscription on the wall of a church in a language with which one was unfamiliar. In such circumstances, one simply does not have the resources to understand it; it will remain there in front of you, enigmatic and beyond your comprehension. This, thinks Danto, is the position of the traditionalist when faced with avant-garde works of art; it is not that the works do not mean anything, it is only that the traditionalist lacks the resources to understand them.

Let me sum up where we have got to so far. Up until the eighteenth century, there was no unified concept of the fine arts. Inasmuch as the word "art" had a stable meaning, it meant something like "skill". During the Enlightenment, a concept of "the fine arts" was developed; they were objects that provided aesthetic experiences and imitated nature. This is the concept to which our traditionalist still adheres. At the beginning of the twentieth century, there was yet another change: a new concept of art developed. Objects were works of art if they somehow were about what it was to be a work of art. Now we can return to the issue with which we started: the debate between the traditionalist and the radical. If the radical is using the modernist concept of art, and the modernist concept of art would count Klein's *Anthropometries* as art, then we would have an explanation of the disagreement. The traditionalist is using one concept of art and the radical another. It would be no surprise that they do not agree about cases.

The next step, then, is to investigate whether the modernist concept of art is in good shape: that is, whether we can allow the radical to rely on it. In doing this, we must be careful to distinguish two questions. Let us put "art" aside for a moment, and consider instead the definition of the word "witch". Ignoring subtleties, the definition of "witch" is "a woman who is in league with the Devil". There are two questions we can ask about this. First, does this definition capture what those people who believe in witches actually believe? Second, is the existence of witches a sensible thing to believe? Let us call a question of the first sort a "descriptive" question; we are merely interested in whether we have *described* some peoples' beliefs accurately. Let us call a question of the second sort an "appropriateness" question; we are interested in whether it is *appropriate* to have such beliefs. In the case of witches, I would say that the answer to the descriptive question is yes and the answer to the appropriateness question is no. Applying this distinction in the case of "art", we can break the question of whether the modernist definition of "art" is adequate into a descriptive question and an appropriateness question. First, is the modernist concept of art an accurate account of what the post-1914 art world really thinks? Second, is it appropriate to have such a concept – does it make any sense? The traditionalist might answer yes to the first question, and no to the second. That is, the traditionalist might think that the art world really does think what the radical claims they think, but also that they have gone horribly wrong in thinking so.

Let us look first at the descriptivist question. The radical claims that there is evidence that they have identified the "new concept of art" correctly: that it is the only way to explain what actually happened in the development of art from the 1860s to the 1960s. The story could be told in various ways but one version would be roughly as follows. Prior to the 1860s, the task of the Old Masters was to peddle illusions: to produce works of art that "imitated beautiful nature". That is, the task was to produce paintings that looked like what they were paintings of. More precisely, they were to provide a visual experience that would match what the spectator would have were they faced with the subject of the painting face to face. In the 1860s, Manet appeared to repudiate this task. He produced paintings that stepped away from three-dimensional illusions; their spatial relations were awry (*A Bar at the Folies-Bergère*) or they looked as if they were a flat surface on which figures had simply been stuck (*Le Déjeuner sur l'herbe*). That is, Manet appeared to be presenting his paintings *as paintings*, rather than windows to another world.

The moral to draw from Manet's revolution was that it was possible to present non-illusionistic paintings and that these still be works of art. That is, he showed by example that being illusionistic was not a necessary condition for being a work of art. The next to come along were the cubists. They produced paintings that lacked perspective; the depth in the painting (if there was depth in the painting) came not from lines that converged on a vanishing point but from a variety of other methods – from the juxtaposition of depicted volumes to the incorporation of actual three-dimensional objects on the canvas. These, too, were art; what the cubists had shown was that it was possible for a painting to lack perspective, or any sense of "realism" in the traditional sense, and still be art. After the cubists there was a move to abstraction. Abstract (or non-figurative) art did not depict anything at all, or at least it did not depict anything you might meet with as you wandered around the world. Hence, paintings did not need to depict objects in the world in order to be art. Without illusion, perspective and figures, what was there left of painting? After the first phase of abstraction, the history of painting seemed to move to a more positive phase. Paintings drew attention to their physical being. Painters such as Frank Stella changed the shape of their paintings and painted in relation to the frame so as to draw attention to the fact that the painting was an object. Jackson Pollock, who threw and dripped his paint on to the canvas, drew attention to the action of painting, repudiating traditional ways of applying paint. Others of the abstract expressionists drew attention to the expanse of canvas, to its literal two-dimensionality.

How can we make sense of this? What account can we give that explains these developments? The modernist account seems tailor-made: Manet, under pressure from both a changing world (and Paris was changing at a faster rate than most) and the easily achieved naturalism of photography, started to explore what it is for a painting to be a painting. The baton passed to the cubists, the abstractionists and then further along the chain, each pushing the exploration a little further. The role that the modernists claim for painting – that of it exploring its own nature – provides the explanation for art history taking the form it did. Hence, the fact that art history did take this form is support for the theory. If a theory implies that the world will be a certain way and, when we check, we find out that the world is indeed that way, that is support for the theory.

Where, according to modernist theory, does it all end? When did art finally uncover its real nature? Opinions differ, but let us return to Danto and Warhol's *Brillo Boxes*, which is where Danto took the end to be. Why there? Recall Danto's claim that Warhol's work was the first to foreground that a work of art could be perceptually indistinguishable from a mere real thing. Art deals in appearances; that is, when *art* explores the nature of art it does so by experimenting to discover whether or not something can lack a perceptual property (such as illusion, perspective or figuration) and remain art. What Warhol showed, according to Danto, was that an object could lack *any* perceptual property that distinguished it from a mere real thing and yet remain art. That truly does seem the end of the line: where could art go from there? There are no more perceptual properties that it could negate.

Let us push this a little further before standing back and seeing whether we can make sense of the whole approach. What happens at the end of the line? Answering this question gives us one version of the division between modernism (the project of self-definition) and postmodernism (whatever comes after). What does come after – according to Danto – is that art no longer has a role: it can be whatever it wants to be. As he says, "It does not matter any longer what you do, which is what pluralism means. When one direction is as good as another direction, there is no concept of direction any longer to apply" (Danto 1986: 115).

This support for modernist theory from the actual course of art history is, on the face of it, rather impressive. It would be as if you had been watching someone over the course of a day and seen them perform various apparently disparate tasks: they go outside and gather berries, they go shopping for sugar, they heat up a load of glass jars and they cook a load of ingredients together in a large pot. Someone comes along and provides an explanation that connects all these together: they are making jam. Similarly, there was a bewildering succession of movements in the avant-garde of twentieth-century art. The modernist comes along and provides an explanation: it was a quest for self-definition. Should we then grant to the modernist that they have at least the descriptive question right – that the concept of art, at some time between the mid-1860s and the early 1900s, did become one of self-definition?

The support from the actual course of art history looks impressive, but we should not allow the modernist to choose which art history to tell us. After all, the modernist seems to leave a lot out. Duchamp was exhibiting objects that were perceptually indistinguishable from mere real things fifty years before Warhol. Where in the modernist story are the Dadaists? The surrealists? The continuous and strong tradition of figurative painting? It would be as if we discovered, of the person we had been watching, that they had not only gone outside and gathered berries, gone shopping for sugar, heated up a load of glass jars, and then cooked a load of ingredients together in a large pot, but they had also put the jars in the recycling, added curry powder to the ingredients, and done a thousand other things besides. In those circumstances, the "theory" of their actions ("they are making jam") looks a great deal less impressive. Similarly, once one adds in the messy details of the art history, the modernist theory looks a great deal less impressive.

To reply to this, the modernist has to argue that they have picked out the *right* history. There is independent reason to exclude those that I have mentioned: the Dadaists, the surrealists and the figurative painters. However, it is difficult to see what that independent reason could be. They could argue that they have identified the *significant* developments in the twentieth-century history of art, but this looks to be circular (it is significant only because it supports modernism). Alternatively, they could make some large-scale value judgements to the effect that Dada, surrealism and figuration have produced no worthwhile works and hence do not merit a mention. However, it would be an ambitious hypothesis to think that all and only the good works of art produced in the twentieth century are those that fit into the modernist paradigm. The claim that, after the turn of the nineteenth century, all significant art fitted into the role of self-definition is starting to look rather implausible.

Recall Danto's "To see something as art requires something the eye cannot descry – an atmosphere of artistic theory, a knowledge of the history of art: an artworld". To revert to the analogy I used in the Introduction, Danto thinks of art along the lines of an ongoing conversation in which people comment on what others have said before. To understand any individual contribution to the conversation, one needs to know what the conversation is about (the "artistic theory") and how it has gone so far ("the history of art"). However, this prompts various questions: whose conversation? Can anyone join in? What of conversations that are happening on the other side of the room?

To show this, let us return to Klein and his *Anthropometries*. Klein has some claim to being an artistic innovator in several of the fields that dominated that post-war avant-garde: monochrome painting, environmental sculpture, non-static art, conceptual art, minimal art, new media, mixed media and performance art (McEvilley 2010: 186). Indeed, the *Anthropometries* have a claim to being the first instance of modern performance art and Iris Clert speculated of an earlier piece of Klein's ("Ritual for the Relinquishing of Immaterial Zones of Pictorial Sensibility") that it was "the first piece of Conceptual Art" (*ibid.*: 142). We might treat these as the exaggerations of the pro-Klein camp, but we can also ask why an arguably important innovator of the avant-garde never gets mentioned in the writings of theoretical modernism.

Note that we have raised two problems for modernism. First, there is some work that does not look as if it fits into their art history, among which we find Dadaism, surrealism and figurative art. Klein is a different problem: he does look as if he fits in somehow, but not very comfortably. Let us look at an episode in his life in a little more detail. The mid-1950s was a boom time for modernism. In New York, the abstract expressionists were at the height of their influence and popularity; Mark Rothko was producing his Four Seasons series of paintings (one of which will be discussed in Chapter 3). Already, however, the "conversation" was moving on. In reaction to the expressive fields of colour, the American artists Robert Ryman and Jasper Johns were producing paintings that either were, or were tending to, undifferentiated monochrome. In 1956, Klein had started producing monochrome paintings: blue canvasses. Superficially, one might take this to be part of the same "conversation"; Klein even had a show at an important New York gallery in 1962.

Klein's New York show was, however, notably unsuccessful – nothing was sold – and the New York art world was dismissive (McEvilley 2010: 170–71). Part of the problem was that Klein did not see his own work as part of the general modernist project of self-definition. For him, at least in as much as we can gauge his state of mind accurately, monochromes had an immense spiritual significance. Klein had some really quite bizarre beliefs, including beliefs about the mystical powers of blue. Instead of being a soldier in the army of self-definition, he thought he was ushering in a new spiritual era. So, if Klein was actually doing what he thought he was doing (we shall look at the relation between intention and interpretation in Chapter 5) then he was not part of the modernist conversation.

The modernist concept of the arts underestimates the complexity of the twentieth-century art world. Arguably, it does give an accurate description of a certain trajectory that ran through the visual arts: a tradition that began with Manet, developed a degree of self-consciousness with Duchamp, and then a great deal of self-consciousness in New York in the 1950s and 1960s (when modernism as a theory started to influence painters' work). However, a lot of other things were going on, some of them related and some of them quite unrelated. Klein is a good example of this complexity. His work looks like modernist work, but it is not part of the "atmosphere of theory"; it does not fit seamlessly into the modernist art world.

Where does that leave our discussion? We thought we had a neat diagnosis of the debate between the traditionalist and the radical: the traditionalist excluded *Anthropometries* on the grounds that it was not made with the intention of provoking the aesthetic experience and the radical included it as being part of modernism. However, we can now see that it is not even clear that it *would* fall under the modernist definition. So are the *Anthropometries* works of art or not? We seem to be back where we started.

Contemporary philosophy of art could step in and attempt to help us out of the impasse. Jerrold Levinson and George Dickie have both provided versions of what are known as "institutional theories" of the arts (these are also known as "procedural theories" or "genetic theories"). These are best understood as attempts to refine the modernist concept of the arts into a formal definition; moreover, a formal definition that attempts not only to cover art since the turn of the nineteenth century, but also (retrospectively) to cover the traditional fine arts. As we have seen, there is a huge variety of objects and events that have been granted the status of art. How are we to find unity in this variety? What could they possibly have in common in virtue of which they have status of art? According to Levinson, "the only universal content [art] now retains" is that art essentially refers to itself (1979: 14). It is worth noting how far we have travelled from the traditionalist's concept of art; we have even dropped the modernist claim that art is concerned with the project of self-definition. All that remains that is essential to the concept is that art in some way refers to itself. We can quickly turn that into a definition: a work of art is an object that stands in the right relation to the institution of art itself. What needs to be clarified is what is meant by "the right relation" and what is meant by "the institution of art".

Both Dickie and Levinson claim that objects are put in the right relation to the institution of art via the intentions of the artist. According to Dickie, someone acting on behalf of the art world puts the object forward "as a candidate for appreciation". Dickie nowhere defines "the art world", although he does describe its various aspects at some length:

> [Its] core personnel ... is a loosely organized, but nevertheless related, set of persons including artists (understood to refer to painters, writers, composers), producers, museum directors, museum goers, theatre goers, reporters for newspapers, critics for publications of all sorts, art historians, art theorists, philosophers of art, and others.
> (Dickie 1974: 35–6)

According to Levinson, an object is a work of art if someone intends that the object be regarded "in any of the ways works of art existing prior to it have been correctly regarded" (Levinson 1979: 6). Hence, for Levinson, the relevant institution of art is all art that has come before; that is, objects that figure in the history of art. At a general level, the theories have the same structure:

what it is to be a work of art is for someone to have intended that the object stand in a certain relation with the institution of art. We can assume that Klein intended his *Anthropometries* to stand in the right relation to the institution of art (either by intending it to be a candidate for appreciation or intending it to be regarded in some of the ways previous works of art have been regarded) so we can assume that it comes out as a work of art.

My worry is not whether such theories can be defended against objection; let me grant that they will capture all and only the huge variety of objects and events that have been granted the status of art. Even if successful, however, there are two reasons why I do not think institutional theories are an enlightening contribution to the debate. First, they are uninformative in that they do not shed any light on the question as I have framed it. Let us return to our example: anyone who is genuinely puzzled as to whether or not *Anthropometries* is a work of art is not puzzled as to whether or not Klein intended the event to stand in the right relation to the art world; that is not what they want to know. The institutional theories definition of "art" is not helpful in sorting out the kinds of puzzlement that drive us towards seeking a definition of art in the first place. The accounts, whatever they are accounts of, are not accounts of whatever is at issue in this debate. The second reason I find them unhelpful lies in their aspiration to range over not only art in the modernist period, but also the pre-modernist traditional arts. It is just about plausible that what makes Duchamp's *Fountain* art, and in that respect distinct from other urinals in the world, is that the former stands in the right relation to the art world or to art history and other urinals do not. However, that simply seems an obtuse thing to say about *The Night Watch*. Institutional theories take a defining feature of the modernist concept of the arts, polish it up, and then apply it to all arts including the pre-modernist arts. However – and unsurprisingly – it does not seem to fit. Whatever it is that makes *The Night Watch* art is surely not that someone intended it to stand in the right relation to an art world.

Where do we go from here? If we have not managed to find a sensible answer to the question as to whether *Anthropometries* is art then perhaps that is because we do not have a sensible question. There are two reasons why we might think we do not have a sensible question. One reason is circumstantial and the other more substantial. Both reasons point in the same direction, however: that sorting out whether or not something is art is not very important.

We have seen already in this chapter that there are at least two concepts of art: the traditionalist concept and the modernist concept. I have gone along with the suggestion that these concepts came into existence in the mid-seventeenth century and the early twentieth century, respectively. The circumstantial evidence that it is not very important whether or not something is art is that there is something a bit odd about concepts "coming into existence" so late in human history. Compare, for example, the concept of "person" or "object". These are concepts that structure our thinking; it is difficult to see how we could get by without them. It is interesting to know what these concepts amount to, which is why philosophers spend so much time thinking about them. Evidently, we got along without the concept of "art" for several hundred years. How important can a concept be if we can manage for so long without it?

The more substantial reason for being sceptical about the importance of sorting out whether or not something is art is that what is at issue is not a simple matter of classification. Let us go back to the first reason I found institutional theories unhelpful: that they do not illuminate what is at issue for people puzzled as to whether works such as *Anthropometries* are art. I said there that anyone who is puzzled is not puzzled about whether, as a matter of fact, the work stands in the right relation to the institution of art. What, then, are they puzzled about?

The amount of heat the discussion tends to generate suggests that what they are worried about is whether *Anthropometries* has a status elevated enough to be called "art". The thought that has been operating throughout this chapter is that if we get a firm grasp of what "art" means, we can sort out this problem. We get a firm grasp of what "art" means by coming up with a theory of art: a substantial analysis of the concept. However, we have also seen that the concept is in a bit of a mess; first we had no concept, then we had the traditionalist concept, and now we have the modernist concept. Different people use the word in different ways. It is no wonder we cannot get a substantial analysis of something that is such a moving target. We might better capture the way things are with a different approach. Let us grant that people use the term "art" in a rough-and-ready way, some more inclined to the traditionalist use and some, the modernist use. Whether they are prepared to apply the word to a particular object is not what matters. What matters instead is whether the object is any good: whether it is interesting, original, provocative, life-affirming, or has some other property that makes it worthy of our attention. Kendall Walton expressed this view in some comments he wrote about Dickie's book:

> Concepts are not mountains. Their mere existence ("in a language")
> does not make them worthy objects of analysis ... I do not think

Dickie's "classificatory" concept of art is very important in our conceptual scheme. It seems to me that critics, especially the better ones, rarely put much weight on the notion of art … What we feel is important about paintings, films, musical works, avant-garde shenanigans – in what ways they are exciting, comforting, intriguing, revealing, upsetting, maddening, or disgusting, for example, and how they are related to each other and other things – can be expressed and understood, not only without stating whether they are art (in Dickie's sense), but without assuming even any implicit understanding about this.   (Walton 1977: 99)

Let us return to the *Anthropometries* and think about what we would like to say about them. The evening began with "The Monotone Symphony", which, as the quotation that heads this chapter says, Klein had conceived of in 1949 (it had been performed previously in 1957) as a counterpart to his monochrome paintings. The "symphony" consisted of a single note played for twenty minutes, followed by twenty minutes of silence. During the first twenty minutes, the models covered themselves in the paint that Klein had patented, International Klein Blue, and pressed themselves against large sheets of paper. Klein subsequently went on to make around two hundred works using the female body as either a means of applying paint, or as a stencil around which to spray paint. Some of these are rather beautiful; beautiful enough, indeed, to perhaps satisfy a naive traditionalist that they might be art. I say "naive traditionalist" because the meaning or significance of the work goes beyond its surface appeal (a point I shall return to presently).

Where, then, should we look for the meaning or significance of the work? Different aspects of the work might be up for debate. What is the significance (if any) of the naked models? (Is Klein's use of their bodies wrong, and, if so, why?) What could be interesting about twenty minutes of a monotone (it is certainly not perceptually interesting)? To what extent was the evening merely provocative? What role, if any, should Klein's adherence to Rosicrucian beliefs play in the interpretation of the work? What relation (if any) is there between this work and later works, such as happenings, the Situationists and Fluxus? We can ask these questions, and argue about their answers, putting aside the sterile issue of whether or not the *Anthropometries* are art.

This answer might prove too radical for some (I confess it is too radical for me). The reason it is too radical is that unless we know the sort of thing we are looking at, we will not know what to look for to answer the questions above. One could imagine an evening such as the one Klein provided that was not art, but pornography. If so, its value will lie in its propensity to provoke sexual excitement. If one instead classifies the event as (for example) therapy, its value will lie in its propensity to cure anxieties. It is only if we can classify it as art that we can identify where to look to decide its value. Thus, it looks as if we are back where we started; we cannot shirk the issue of whether or not *Anthropometries* is art.

There is, however, an alternative that has been suggested in some recent (and forthcoming) work by Dominic Lopes. This seems to allow us to accept that "art" is too much of a moving target to define, without leaving us empty handed when it comes to classifying objects and thus knowing how to interpret them (nothing Walton says suggests he would disagree; indeed, other of his work suggests the kind of approach Lopes takes (Walton 1987)). We can accept that we have a rough-and-ready, much contested grasp of the word "art" *and* that the interesting divide is not between things that are art and things that are not art. However, there are other divides that *are* interesting: between things that are paintings, things that are sculptures, things that are happenings, things that are ready-mades, things that are in no art form whatsoever, and so on and so forth (Lopes 2008).

As we have seen, the question as to whether the *Anthropometries* is art gave us no traction; we did not seem to be able to say anything that was interesting and true and that addressed the issues we wanted to address. Lopes's suggestion is that instead we attempt to identify the art form of which *Anthropometries* is an instance: does it fall under painting, music or something else? If it does not fall under an existing art form, is it pioneering a new art form? Where does asking such questions leave the debate between the traditionalist and the modernist? The traditionalist could perhaps be persuaded to see the *Anthropometries* as an instance of an existing art form and evaluate it as that (although the evaluation will probably not be favourable). It is more likely that the traditionalist will continue to regard it as a joke and deny both that it falls under an existing art form or that it is pioneering a new art form. The modernist will face the same questions: having to decide whether it falls under an existing art form (and defend it as an instance of that) or argue that it is pioneering a new art form (and will have to come up with some story about that).

This approach delivers three immediate advantages. The first is that, unlike the question "Is it art?", the question as to whether an object belongs to an existing art form or is pioneering a new art form does not look empty. All sides can agree that the *Anthropometries* is not (for example) a painting, although the results could be paintings and the event could be a way of producing paintings (set to music). Attempting to decide the form the event *does* fall under will be more difficult, although the interlocutors are not left with nothing to discuss. Is the event, together with other events that came later, part of a new art form – the happening? Or is the event a work of conceptual art? What relevant properties do they have in common (or lack) that would decide the issue? The second advantage, which is a strong argument for this approach, is that unlike institutional theories this approach sorts out the debate between the traditionalist and the modernist in the right way. As we saw above, one reason for rejecting those theories was that they took an essentially modernist view and attempted to apply it retrospectively to everything. If what is up for grabs in the debate between the traditionalist and the modernist is a theory of art – *all* art – then what is said about the *Anthropometries* applies equally to *The Night Watch*. According to Lopes, the debate is *not* about all art; the debate is about whether the *Anthropometries* belong to an art form and, if so, which one. This is entirely irrelevant to anything we might want to say about *The Night Watch* (unless the *Anthropometries* turns out to be a painting), which seems exactly the right result. Finally, the approach helps us make sense of interpretation. Above, I suggested that we have to know what something is in order to be able to make sense of it. Making sense of something as pornography is a different matter from making sense of something as therapy, which in turn is a different matter from making sense of something as falling under a particular art form. Lopes suggests that, instead of attempting to makes sense of something as *art*, we attempt to make sense of it as a *painting*, or *conceptual art*. This is helpful as, in general, the more specific the category under which we try to make sense of something the better. Understanding something as a dog will, in general, be more illuminating than understanding something as an animal. Similarly, understanding something as an instance of an art form will be more illuminating than understanding something as art.

2. THE VALUE OF ART

Lucian Freud's *Hotel Bedroom*

The complaint of the traditionalist of the previous chapter can perhaps be summed up as the claim that much art since Duchamp's *Fountain* is not worth attending to: that is, a great deal of modern and contemporary art simply is not valuable. As we saw, we could not answer the question "But is it art?" until we had a better grasp of what it was that was at issue in asking the question. For analogous reasons, we cannot answer the question "But is it valuable?" until we have a better grasp of what it is for a work of art to be valuable. Indeed, we have to start a little further back even than that. For we cannot grasp what it is for art to be valuable until we have some grasp of what it is for anything to be valuable: that is, some grasp of the nature of value.

For some people, nihilists, nothing is of value. For others, the only things that are of value are human experiences. For yet others, there are plenty of things that are of value. This is a messy and complicated part of philosophy, and going into it will not tell us anything distinctive about art as whatever we conclude will apply to everything valuable, not only to art. So I am going to presuppose that works of art, like many other things, are candidates for being valuable. It will then be up to art critics to sort those works of art that are valuable from the ones that are not. My discussion will concern the kind of value this might be. Before that, however, I need to establish two things about value.

The first thing to establish is that there is a difference between an object possessing instrumental value and it possessing final value. I use the term "object" very broadly to encompass things, processes and events. I use the term "final value" where others might use the term "intrinsic value"; all I mean by "final value" is that the value of the object is non-instrumental. What, then, is it for an object to possess instrumental value? Some objects are useful to us for getting hold of something else that really is valuable: that is, they are instruments for our getting something we value. Let us assume that it is valuable for us to be in Bristol. The coach is useful for us to get to Bristol. In this scenario, the coach is instrumentally valuable; it is an instrument for our getting something we value. Of course, what we are getting might itself only be instrumentally valuable. We might only value being in Bristol so that we can attend a job interview. Furthermore, attending the job interview itself is likely to be instrumentally valuable: as the means of getting a job. At the end of the chain, however, there will be something that we do not value only as a means of getting something else and this, whatever it is, has "final value" for us.

Let us examine three characteristics of instrumental value that will be relevant to our discussion. The first and most obvious is that an object is instrumentally valuable if it is a means to some valuable end where that end can be described independently of the means. Consider, for example, the coach journey to Bristol. If the desired end is *being in Bristol* then the coach journey has only instrumental value: it is a means to an end. However, if the end cannot be spelled out independently – that is, if what we really value is not *being in Bristol* but *being in Bristol having got there by coach* – then the coach journey is not merely a means to an end, but part of that end. In other words, it is not merely a means to getting what we value, but part of what we value, part of the final value. To be truly an instrumental value, the value must be a means to the end, and not part of that end. The second characteristic is that the instrumental value of an object is "inherited" from the final value to which it is a means. Taken in itself, the object that is instrumentally valuable might not be valuable. It might even be a real nuisance; you might be one of those people who hate coach journeys. The instrumental value it has is only that of being a means to something that you do find valuable: being in Bristol. Even things that are terribly dull, painful or tedious can have instrumental value. Visiting the dentist might not be something we look forward to, but many of us do it anyway as it is a means to a greater good. The third characteristic is that if something has only instrumental value for us – that is, we value it only as a means to some end – then, should a more efficient way of achieving that end come along, it makes sense for us to exchange the previous means to the end for the more efficient means. For example, if it turns out that the train is a cheaper, easier and more pleasurable way to get to Bristol, then it makes sense to exchange getting to Bristol by coach for getting to Bristol by train.

The second thing about value we need to establish is the difference between something simply having a value, and something having a value as the kind of thing it is. A screwdriver might have a value for propping open a door but that is not the value it has *as a screwdriver*. The value it has as a screwdriver will be the value it has for screwing in screws. We can be neutral about what makes this its value as a screwdriver; it might be *the value it has performing the function its makers intended it to perform*, or *the value it has performing the function it is generally used to perform*, or even some other candidate. Whatever determines that value, it has a value as a screwdriver which is different from the value it has as something else, such as its value *as a doorstop, a paperweight* or *a Christmas present*. Similarly, I shall go on to argue, there is a difference between a painting simply having a value and it having a value *as a painting*.

The work of art I am going to consider in this chapter is Lucian Freud's painting *Hotel Bedroom*. Freud (1922–2011) was a British painter – grandson of Sigmund Freud – who has, in the main, painted the human figure. In that respect this painting is unusual, depicting, as it does, a dramatic situation. It was painted in Paris in 1954 and the two figures are Freud himself and his then wife, Caroline Blackwood. They had been married for a year. The marriage did not last; after two further years of alcohol-fuelled excess, Blackwood left. In this chapter I shall try to throw light on what we mean when we claim that this is – as I believe it is – a wonderful painting. What exactly is the nature of this painting's – and other paintings' – value?

I shall start off with an intuitively appealing line of thought that suggests that the value of the painting is the value that it has for certain individuals. One might divide the world broadly into the objective and the subjective. Matters are objective if they are about the way things actually are. That I have a desk in front of me is an objective matter, as are Paris being the capital of France, Napoleon Bonaparte being dead and ten being greater than five. Matters are subjective if they are (to put it loosely) a matter of opinion. That broccoli is nicer than sprouts, that beach holidays are more relaxing than traipsing around monuments and that Churchill was the greatest ever Englishman are all subjective. Now consider the proposition that *Hotel Bedroom* is a wonderful work of art. Is that objective or subjective? Those who think it is subjective might back up their view by saying that whether or not you think it is wonderful is a matter of opinion. Some people like that sort of thing, and some people do not. For those who like that sort of thing the picture may well be wonderful; for those who do not, it will not.

The strength of this argument will be tested throughout this chapter. Rather than address it directly, I shall start by looking at the sheer variety of values the painting might have. Once one starts to think about it, the different kinds of value can appear endless. There is nothing peculiar in this; as we saw above, even the humble screwdriver can have several kinds of value. To change the example, a bottle of wine has all kinds of value: monetary value, investment value, gustatory value and even, in some bizarre circumstance, value as a weapon. How do we isolate, among all these different kinds of value, the value it has *as a bottle of wine*? A painting might have similar kinds of value: certainly, monetary value and investment value, but also trivial kinds of value such as covering a damp patch on the wall and even being valuable as something with which to hit burglars. However, valuing a painting for these reasons is not valuing it *as a painting*. The value of a bottle of wine as a bottle of wine is, presumably, the value of the pleasure it affords when consumed in the appropriate manner. What we shall do in this chapter is to find the analogous answer for painting: what is it to value a painting *as a painting*? Or, to be more particular, what is it to value *Hotel Bedroom* as a painting?

Even if we do find an answer to this we shall not have a general answer to the question of what it is to value a work of art *as a work of art*. As we saw in the previous chapter, we have reason to be sceptical about the classification "art". In the same way as there is not a definition that covers all those things that anyone calls "art", there will not be a value that is distinctive to all those things that anyone calls "art" (Lopes 2008). This, I think, is roughly right and I shall return to discuss the point at the end of the chapter. For the moment, however, let us focus on finding what it is to value *Hotel Bedroom* as a painting.

I shall begin by ignoring the outlying kinds of value and looking at those that seem serious candidates for being the answer to our question. Let us start at the obvious place; that paintings (or, at least, paintings such as *Hotel Bedroom*) capture the appearance of the world. That is, paintings can teach us about the way the world looks. Here is one way of interpreting that claim. Paintings might have value as sources of information. *Hotel Bedroom*, for example, is a self-portrait of Lucian Freud and his wife at a time when their marriage was unhappy. The claim I am putting forward for consideration is that the value of the painting lies in the information it conveys: information about, for example, the health (or otherwise) of the Freud–Blackwood marriage (one does not have to be portentous – the information it conveys could merely be information about how people dressed in the 1950s). Is valuing *Hotel Bedroom* as a source of information valuing the painting *as a painting*?

To value a painting as a source of information about a marriage would be to accord it instrumental value. That is, the painting is a means to some end that we really value: some items of information. Paintings can have this value; indeed, it is fairly certain that some paintings do. Holbein's paintings are, apparently, the best source of information about the clothes fashions of the Tudor court. The question is whether this instrumental value is the value we accord a painting *as a painting* (I shall take it for granted in what follows that we are talking about the value of *Hotel Bedroom* as a painting).

The view being put forward is that the value of *Hotel Bedroom* is an instrumental value: what we really value is the information the painting conveys – information about the Freud marriage. It has the first characteristic of instrumental value: the valued end – the information – can be specified independently of the means. The next two characteristics of instrumental value bring out how counter-intuitive this is. The value the painting had would be exhausted by its conveying the information in the same way as the value of the coach journey would be exhausted by its getting us to Bristol. Once we have reached Bristol, the coach journey is no longer valuable to us. Analogously, once we have the information the painting would no longer be valuable to us. However, this is not how we think about paintings. We do not class them in the same category as shopping lists or notes to the milkman: things whose value is exhausted once their information is conveyed. Rather, we return to paintings again and again. We might even visit galleries to seek out our favourite paintings: paintings we know well. Such behaviour would be quite inexplicable if the value of a painting was an instrumental value. The final characteristic of instrumental value is even more counter-intuitive. If the value of *Hotel Bedroom* were an instrumental value then, if there were another object that was a better source of information about the Freud marriage (say a diary), we should exchange the painting for that object. Again, this is not how we think about paintings; *Hotel Bedroom* would not cease to have the value it has were the relevant diary to be discovered. We can conclude from this that the value of *Hotel Bedroom* does not lie in the information it conveys.

To identify the kind of value *Hotel Bedroom* has we clearly need to distance ourselves from valuing it as a vehicle for information. Rather than being a vehicle of information, perhaps the value of a painting is that, in some sort of way, it does us good. That is, the value of *Hotel Bedroom* is in the beneficial effects that it has on its spectators. There is something right and something wrong about this thought. To sort the issues out, we need to settle what sorts of effect we are talking about. I shall consider three.

Above, I considered the view that equates the value of a painting, for a person, with whether or not he or she likes it. I am going to assume that whether or not one likes something is a matter of the effect is has on one;

that is, whether or not it gives one pleasure. Before considering that view, I shall consider the other two sorts of effect a painting might have on us. The first sort is a hodgepodge of effects that broadly go under the name "therapy" and the second is the effect of providing decoration for a room. What, then, would it be for a painting to be valuable as therapy? The broad thought – as I said above – is that a painting is valuable to the extent that it does us good. At one extreme, the value of a particular painting might be the contribution it makes to some person's mental health. One can imagine a case in which someone is particularly depressed or anxious and a certain painting might calm them down. This is unlikely to be *Hotel Bedroom* with its rather fraught subject matter; however, there are paintings (perhaps Raoul Dufy's colourful beach scenes of Nice) that are more plausible candidates for this effect.

It is not usually the *consumption* of paintings that is thought to have this value, but their *production*. That is, a painting is valuable to the extent that it does the person producing the painting good. Once again this covers a huge variety of cases. It is thought (surely rightly) that it is a good thing to encourage small children to "be creative": to produce paintings, drawings, sketches, skits and plays for the sake of their mental development. There is also a form of psychotherapy that uses art and the creation of art as a means of expression and communication; this, for obvious reasons, is particularly valuable for those who have problems expressing themselves verbally.

Recall, I am not denying that paintings – or at least some paintings – are valuable for these reasons. The question is whether this is their value when considered *as paintings*. Something about this answer seems right. It is often said that artists create in response to a kind of natural urge; they feel the need to paint welling up inside them such that they cannot help but produce art. Paintings become things in the world that are the products of mental activity, and get their value by being an expression of that mental activity or an attempt to communicate that mental activity. Psychoanalytic accounts of creativity stress this. Hanna Segal (a student of Melanie Klein) has put forward the view that creativity is a matter of "reparation": an attempt to restore a psychic wholeness that was destroyed during what Klein referred to as "the depressive position" (Segal 2004: 44). If this is true, then the value of art – the value of paintings as paintings – is in the beneficial effects they have on our mental lives. It might be true, indeed I think it is true, that at least part of the explanation of why we create art lies deep in the complicated and sometimes traumatic history of our psychological development. For some people, the alternative to creating art would be unhappiness and possibly insanity (Wollheim 1986: ch. VII).

Let us characterize the basic explanation roughly as: a work of art is valuable to the extent that it contributed to the psychological well-being of the artist. A little thought will show that this cannot be an account of the value of a painting as a painting. That the painting relieved the artist's mind is something that happened at its creation, while its value is something that is manifest for as long as the painting exists. This implausibility of the claim surfaces in a number of different ways. To see this, compare *Hotel Bedroom* (which, let us assume, is a good painting) with William-Adolphe Bouguereau's *Abduction of Psyche* (which, let us assume for the sake of argument, is not a good painting).

There are at least three ways in which identifying the value of a painting with the value of contributing to the artist's well-being is problematic. Whatever else we want to say about the value of a painting as a painting, let us agree that it must have something to do with the way the painting looks. To improve the value of a painting, we need to improve its looks; to diminish the value, we need to degrade its looks. This theory claims that the greater the contribution to well-being, the greater the value. However, that would only be true if the greater the contribution to well-being, the better a painting looked. The problem (the first problem) is that it is not true, or at least not always true. We cannot always tell, just by looking at them side by side, which of Freud's or Bouguereau's paintings have had the greatest net contribution to psychological well-being. The value of a painting should be something we can find out by experiencing the way it looks, not some hidden fact about it. The second problem is related: the goal of psychological health is not necessarily the same as the goal of producing a painting that is valuable as a painting. The point of art-therapy classes is to produce something that will aid psychological well-being; if it turns out to have a valuable appearance that will be an additional extra.

The third problem for this account is the same as the problem faced by the one that gave the value of a painting in terms of being a source of information: it construes the value of a painting as an instrumental value when it is not. We can specify the end (the improvement in the artist's psychological health) independently of the means. As we saw above, this has two implausible consequences. First, once that end has been achieved (the artist's psychological health has been improved) the painting no longer has any value. Second, were we to find a more efficient way of improving the artist's psychological health then it would make sense for us to substitute that way for the painting. However, as we have seen, both these results are counterintuitive. The value of *Hotel Bedroom* is not so easily exhausted, and we do not regard its value as being equally or better captured by something else; it is not so easily substituted.

As I said above, it is plausible that artists are frequently driven from what lies deep in their psychology. This fact, if it is a fact, would be generally true of paintings. It is a good and surprisingly useful rule of thumb that any consideration that applies to all painting (or to all art) cannot be used to explain the value of a particular painting (or a particular work of art). All this leaves open the possibility that the way the artist's psychology is *manifest* in the painting may be part of its value as a painting. As we shall see presently, this is part of the account of the value of paintings that I favour.

Let us look at a second effect that might explain the value of paintings: the value they have as decoration. Rooms, especially large public rooms, can look very drab without something on the wall. The claim is that the value of a painting as a painting is its value in – to put it bluntly – brightening up the place. It is certainly true (to reiterate what was said above) that this is one value a painting can have. The question is whether this is the value of a painting as a painting. My hunch is that many people think it is. It is certainly more defensible than the account we have just considered as it is plausible that a painting's value as decoration is linked to the way the painting looks.

The difference between the value a painting might have as decoration and the value it might have as a painting is vividly illustrated in the story of Mark Rothko's commission for a series of paintings to decorate the Four Seasons Restaurant. In 1958, Rothko was well known for large non-figurative paintings that characteristically contained a number of fields of colour. The commission was for "500 to 600 square feet of paintings", which would decorate one of the dining rooms in what was, at the time, the most expensive and exclusive restaurant in New York. *Prima facie*, Rothko's paintings are ideal candidates to decorate a room: they are big and – putting aside the more obviously sombre ones – their colours tend to overwhelm the senses. Indeed, prints of Rothko's paintings (rarely to scale) or prints of Rothko-like paintings can be found on the walls of many a restaurant, living room or bedroom. Two years after agreeing to the contract, Rothko pulled out. Since agreeing, he had experienced a series of doubts. He is reported as saying, "I hope to ruin the appetite of every son of a bitch who ever eats in that room". Later, someone else reported, "He had no intention of handing over his pictures as decorations for parties" (quoted in Breslin 1993: 376, 407).

It is clear that Rothko did not equate the value of his paintings with decoration. What is less clear is what he did think of the value of his paintings (and, as we shall see in Chapter 5, it is not obvious that the artist is the best authority on this question). Indeed, Rothko is one of those painters who tend to inspire, in Robert Hughes's words, "muffled threnodies to the ineffable" (Hughes 1991: 240). Whatever we think is the value of Rothko's paintings, part of what was bothering Rothko was that providing decoration is the wrong candidate for being the value of art. It is difficult to see how one can generate a *substantial* value for painting if it is merely one arm of the interior decoration business. Rothko and Rothko's critics think the paintings have a value greater than merely decorative value. It was because their value as art came into conflict with their value as decoration that Rothko withdrew from his commission to decorate the restaurant.

The above only counts against the account of the value of a painting as decoration if we can make good the claim that it does possess a more substantial value; I hope to do that below. As for the claim that the value of a painting as a painting is its value as decoration, we can see that it suffers from the same flaw as the previous two: it makes the value of a painting as a painting instrumental. The value of the painting is its value in decorating a room. If some more effective means were found of decorating the room then we would substitute those means for the painting. However, this is not how we think of the value of paintings; Rothko's paintings would not only have value in the absence of a more decorative alternative. Of course, that is how the person responsible for decorating the restaurant might have seen it; however, that shows only that such a person would not be valuing the paintings as paintings.

I now get to the final sort of effect I shall consider: namely, a painting is valuable for a person because it gives that person pleasure (or, in other words, because they like it). This has the agreeable consequence (for some) that there is no arguing about taste. If *Hotel Bedroom* gives me pleasure, then I value it. If it does not give you pleasure, then you do not value it. Arguing about whether or not it *really* is valuable would make as much sense as arguing about whether ice cream (which let us suppose gives me pleasure but does not give you pleasure) *really* is nice. In both cases – so this theory would claim – the only sensible thing to do is to agree to differ. Let us call this the "hedonistic theory".

Popular as it is, I do not think this is the correct account of the value we attribute to paintings; that is, I think those who believe this view are mistaken about their own attitude to paintings. So what is wrong with the hedonistic theory? The first error is that there are occasions on which we recognize a difference between *liking* something and *valuing* something, and engaging with art is one of those occasions. There are plenty of films I like that I do not think are particularly valuable as films, and plenty of films I think are valuable as films that I do not particularly like. The same goes for paintings. Indeed, *Hotel Bedroom* is not a painting that gives me much pleasure: the situation it depicts is too bleak and the people too unhappy. I do, however, think it is a valuable painting.

The difference between merely liking something (i.e. getting pleasure from it) and valuing it is apparent when we consider the role of *understanding*. Let us change the example. Suppose that Josh is a cricket aficionado: he is able to follow the ebb and flow of a game, appreciate why a captain would set a particular field or make a particular bowling change, see that a game could get more exciting the less there seems to be happening, or why a draw could be a brilliant result. Suppose that Jim is not a cricket aficionado: he understands none of these things. On the other hand, he does like to wander down to the ground at the end of the day as he likes the look of all these people dressed in white walking around with apparent purpose. Josh and Jim both like the game; each of them gets pleasure from watching it. However, if we ask ourselves which of them values cricket as cricket the answer is surely that only Josh does. Jim values it as a pleasant spectacle, but that is not to value it *as cricket*. The difference is that Josh understands the game. He appreciates why a game has the structure it does and can tell a good game from a bad game. Jim might also prefer some games to others (e.g. he might not get as much pleasure from games played in coloured kit under lights) but whether the game is good as cricket makes no difference to him as it is not something he would notice.

The same is true of art. There are some people – the Joshes of the art world – who understand art. There are other people – the Jims of the art world – who do not understand art, even if they like some works of art and dislike others. We are all, I guess, a mixture of the two: we understand some works of art and do not understand others. We can push the analogy further. If someone, let us call her Jill, wanted to discuss cricket there would be no point in her talking to Jim. There is nothing he could say about why a game went the way it did, what the good decisions were, what the bad decisions were, and whether it was a good game. All Jim could say was whether or not he liked it and why he liked it, although his reason for liking it is not based on any understanding of the game. Josh could point to facts about the game – an expertly judged declaration, an overly defensive field, a gritty last wicket stand to force a draw – that would add up to a convincing case for it being a good game. This is the crucial point. In such a conversation, Josh can support his judgement that the game was a good game by appeal to reasons. If Jill wants to argue that it was not a good game, she will have to engage with these reasons. It is not an option for her to say to Josh, "I agree with everything that you are saying but I just do not think it was a good game". Josh will simply be perplexed; anyone who understands cricket would know that the game that had the features he has pointed out was a good game or, if they did not think it was a good game, they would need to come up with a pretty good explanation as to why it was not a good game.

Understanding the game enables Josh to justify his evaluation of the game as good. Similarly, understanding the painting enables us to justify our evaluation of the painting as valuable. We shall look into what those reasons could be in a moment but the mere fact that reasons have a role opens up the possibility of escaping the argument that evaluations of art are subjective. Typically, reasons are general. When Josh gave his reasons for thinking the game was a good game, those were not reasons for *him* alone to think the game was good; they were reasons for *anyone* to think the game was good. If understanding gives us reasons, and reasons are reasons for everyone, then we are able to defend our judgements on works of art. It is not merely a matter of opinion; there is disputing about taste.

What would such a justificatory story be like in the case of painting? We can put together the elements we have already. First, the value of *Hotel Bedroom* as a painting has to be something to do with the way it looks. Furthermore, the value of the painting is not an instrumental value; the painting is not a means to some independently specifiable end. Instead, the value of the painting lies in the viewer's experience *of that very painting*; if we substitute the painting for something else, we get a different value. Finally, as with the experience of a game of cricket, in order to count as valuing the painting as a painting, the experience needs to be based in understanding. In short, we get the following: the value of a painting is the non-instrumentally valuable experience of that painting, where that experience is based in an understanding of the painting (Budd 1995: ch. 1).

With this as our account of the value of paintings as paintings, we can say a little about how we would defend a positive judgement on a particular painting. The reasons for a painting being valuable will include facts about the scene depicted and facts about the way the scene is depicted. Here is the kind of story that could be told to justify the claim that *Hotel Bedroom* is a wonderful painting. It captures a moment of intense emotional complexity. The woman is lying, unhappy, on the bed. Her eyes are directed upwards, but her gaze is directed inwards. The male figure is looking at her. His expression is difficult to read; he is clearly distanced from her, yet his expression is compassionate. The apparent emptiness of their relationship is echoed in the empty rooms in the hotel through the window. The emotional content of the painting is due, in part, to the muted tonal range. Although very much a contemporary scene, the painting has a timeless feel. This is due, in part, to the colour scheme (more reminiscent of past rather than modern masters), the formal layout and the symbolism; as we shall see in Chapter 8, Balthus also draws on the tradition of using a bowl to symbolize female sexuality (in this painting something outside the room). Furthermore, much can be said about the more formal features of the painting: there are no "dead" parts to it, each brushstroke contributes something, there is no redundancy. I shall say a little more below about reasons to which we can appeal to justify our claim that a painting is valuable, but this brief account will suffice for the moment.

If the above justification does carry weight, then anyone who experiences the painting with understanding will have a non-instrumentally valuable experience of it. What exactly is valuable about the experience is given in paragraphs such as the one above. Such accounts would give substance to the argument between someone who thought the painting wonderful, and someone who did not. There is plenty here that could be asserted, debated about or denied; it is not merely an expression of differing preferences. In short, the hedonistic theory is right that we cannot argue about preferences. It is wrong to conclude that we cannot therefore argue about art. Engaging with art as art is not a matter of merely exercising our preferences; it is a matter of trying to understand the work. Understanding the work brings in reasons; reasons that people can use to defend their judgements about works of art.

Does this mean, then, that all disagreements about the value of particular works can be resolved? I do not think it does (here, as elsewhere in this chapter, I draw heavily on Budd 1995: ch. 1). First, there could be more than one understanding of a work that was both correct and complete. An uncontroversial example is difficult to find, as the claim that there is a uniquely correct and complete understanding is compatible with the claim that the meaning of a work might be ambiguous or indeterminate. Nonetheless, if there were more than one understanding of a work that was both complete and correct, this would explain some aesthetic disagreement.

Second, even if there were, for each work, a uniquely correct and complete understanding, that might support incompatible evaluations. That is, one person might take another person to have understood the work correctly, but disagree that the understanding provides reasons for the evaluation. The hedonist might sense a concession here; if two people agree on the understanding of a work but disagree on its evaluation and nothing more can be said then we have a situation of "blameless disagreement". However, it is not the case that nothing more can be said. The two antagonists can discuss their reasons for taking their understanding to support their evaluation. Even if it is unlikely that the argument could be settled, there is no pressure to retreat to the view that "there is no arguing about taste". Consider an example, this time from literature. Two people might agree on their understanding of D. H. Lawrence's *Sons and Lovers*. However, one could take the position Wyndham Lewis argued for in *Paleface*: that Lawrence's valorization of feeling over intellect, primitivism over sophistication, is immature. The other might take the Leavisite position that such matters are indicative of Lawrence's integrity and moral seriousness. This is a substantial disagreement: nothing like a difference in preferences.

Third, apparent aesthetic disagreement could stem from at least one of the parties having a correct understanding but an incorrect evaluation. Sentimentality, or an immaturity of taste, might lead to an overvaluation of things such as the pace of the narrative and an underevaluation of psychological characterization. Alternatively, to take a case from the visual arts, someone might understand a picture correctly, in its full art-historical context, but overrate the importance of the project in which the artist was engaged. That a particular work marked the next development in some branch of the avant-garde is no reason to place a high value on it if there is little value in developing that school of the avant-garde.

In summary, if our judgements on the value of a work of art were simply judgements about what we liked or disliked, there would be no arguing about art. However, because judging the value of a work of art as a work of art is a judgement based on our understanding of the work, there is plenty of scope for reasoned argument. This does not mean, however, that all judgements could be resolved; there is no reason to think that we all ought to agree about everything.

I said above that I would return to the question of the sorts of reasons to which we can appeal to justify our judgement that a painting is valuable. The reasons I gave above emerged out of three considerations: they needed to concern how the painting looks, they needed to be reasons why the experience was non-instrumentally valuable and they needed to constitute an understanding of the painting. I moved quickly from those considerations to talking about the depicted scene and the way the scene had been depicted. I shall finish this chapter by talking about two ways in which this rather narrow conception of reasons relevant to value could be challenged.

The first way to challenge the narrowness of the conception of reasons I favour is to point out that it appears to miss some things that are obviously valuable about works of art. That is, there are things about a work of art that would make it valuable as that work of art which seem to have nothing to do with the way it looks. Principal among these is the place a work has against a background of other works. One example of this is a work's originality; that this was the first work to do things in this particular way is surely something valuable about it. Another work that followed in this tradition would not be as valuable because it was not the first, the original (we shall take up this discussion in Chapter 4). There are other considerations besides originality. Arguably, something that contributes to the value of *Hotel Bedroom* is that it is one of the pivotal works that mark a change in Freud's style. The value of the painting partly consists in the contribution it makes to our understanding Freud's *oeuvre*. Understanding the painting enables us to have a better understanding of the development of his style and perhaps a better understanding of his later paintings. However, this is a fact about *the place* Hotel Bedroom *has in the series of Freud's paintings*, not a fact about *the way the painting looks*.

There are two replies one could make to this. The first would be concessive. We could weaken the condition that nothing counts as a justification for the value of a painting unless it is a reason to experience it in a particular way. That is, we could concede that one of the things that makes *Hotel Bedroom* valuable as a painting is it marking a transition in Freud's style. One of the things that makes Jackson Pollock's "drip paintings" valuable is that nobody had created a work in that way before. (Parenthetically, I should remark that the claim that this is the *only* thing valuable about Pollock's drip paintings – "anyone can do them, but he did them first" – is hopeless; if they are really such that anyone could do them, they are not valuable as paintings.) Whether or not to make this concession might be merely a matter of a difference in how we want to use our words. A painting might be valuable for a number of reasons; the issue is whether the value to be had from experiencing it with understanding is an *important distinctive* value. Provided we all agree that it is an important distinctive value, then it does not matter very much whether you include other things alongside it under being valuable as a painting, and I do not. We agree on the facts of the matter (it is an important distinctive value); we only disagree about what else is classified along with it.

The second reply introduces a complexity into the debate. Having introduced the complexity, the door opens to another way in which the value of painting can be justified. The complexity is to deny that there is an easy distinction to be drawn between those things that are part of our experience and those things that are not part of our experience. Imagine that you can see a dog snarling at you from behind a low wall. What can you actually see and what do you infer from what you see? Here is a possible answer: you see a dog and a wall, and you infer that the dog is dangerous. Perhaps that is already building too much into the experience; perhaps what you see are only *parts* of the dog (only those parts not obscured by the wall) and you infer that it is a whole dog. Even that might be assuming too much. Perhaps you only see coloured patches shaped like a part of a dog, and coloured patches shaped like a wall, and you infer that you are faced with a dog behind a wall. That is, perhaps all we *really* see are coloured patches. Such a claim might have a role in some scientific explanation of our visual systems. That is, there might be a stage in our visual processing that is best described in terms of something like coloured patches. That is not our question, however. What we want to know is the most appropriate description of what we can see, *once our perceptions are in the kind of state where we can make use of them.* Clearly, as I look out of my window I do not simply see patches of colour (in fact, trying to see the world as patches of colour takes quite an effort). Rather, I see sheds, walls, trains and trees.

Let us return to the dog behind the wall and agree that that is what we see: a dog behind a wall. What else do we see? We see the dog snarling. Do we see that the dog is dangerous? It is difficult to know how to answer this question. The answer I want to give is to say that I see the dog is dangerous if the dangerousness of the dog is visible. However, that raises exactly the same question posed in a different form: is the dangerousness of the dog visible? One option here is to adopt the following. If we do not need to do anything *extra* to form a belief on the basis of our experience, then the content of that belief counts as the content of the experience. For example, I might need to do something extra to form the belief that the dog is a Rhodesian Ridgeback. I notice it has certain markings and have to rack my brains to remember which species of dog it is that has those markings. In such a case I do not see that it is a Rhodesian Ridgeback (of course, if I were adept at recognizing species of dog I might simply see that it is a Rhodesian Ridgeback). Do I need to do anything extra to believe that the dog is dangerous? No: it is a big dog, with big teeth, and it is snarling at me. I simply see that the dog is dangerous.

Let us see where we are so far. I have argued that the reasons why a painting is valuable are to do with how the painting looks (i.e. reasons for valuing our experience of the painting). The challenge was from those who think there are reasons why a painting is valuable that have nothing to do with how it looks: for example, its originality, or the place it has in a painter's *oeuvre*. We can now – to an extent, at least – meet this challenge. The challenge relies on a narrow view of how things look. If we take the broader view – that, provided we do not need to do anything extra to form the belief on the basis of our experience, the content of our belief counts as the content of our experience – then we can see a lot more in the painting. In particular, we might not have to do anything *extra* to see Freud's painting as original, or to see its place in his *oeuvre*. Indeed, we might see not only the originality and the changing style, but Freud's anger or disappointment, or the loneliness. So we line up what we see with what we do not need to do anything extra to believe, and what we do not see with what we do need to do something extra to believe. Plausibly, this gets things right: what we can see is part of the value of the painting as a painting, and what we have to work out is not part of the value of the painting as a painting.

You might be wondering how all this helps sort out disagreement as to a picture's value. Suppose I say that one reason why *Hotel Bedroom* is such a wonderful painting is that you can see the tension in it. You say that you cannot see the tension in it (at best, you might say, you can infer it depicts a tense situation because of your background knowledge about Freud's life at the time). Hence, our disagreement as to whether the painting is wonderful for this reason is a disagreement about what can be seen in the painting. Is there any way this can be resolved, or are we simply left at loggerheads? Which of us is right depends on whether, if you looked at the painting with full understanding, you would be able to see the tension in it. How do we know that full understanding will have this result? How do we know whether tension is the kind of thing that can be seen in paintings?

It is difficult to see what we can say about this in general. Some paintings are such that we can see the tension in them and some paintings are not. It all depends on the painting. Hence, we need to consider the question on a case-by-case basis. That is, we need to ask ourselves, when we look at a painting with understanding, whether we need to do anything extra to form a belief about something, or whether we can simply see that something in the picture. Richard Wollheim gives an example of how this might go:

> Consider the following experiment. I look at a picture that includes a classical landscape with ruins. And now imagine the following dialogue: "Can you see the columns?" "Yes." "Can you see the columns as coming from a temple?" "Yes." "Can you see the columns that come from the temple as having been thrown down?" "Yes." "Can

you see them as having been thrown down some hundreds of years ago by barbarians?" "Yes." "Can you see them as having been thrown down some hundreds of years ago by barbarians wearing the skins of asses?" (Pause.) "No." ... Now, let us assume that this spectator is the suitable spectator for this picture. In that case we can understand the "No" as a refusal on his part to be forced beyond the appropriate experience, hence a refusal to force upon the picture something that it does not represent.   (Wollheim 2001: 23–4)

In short, if a "suitable spectator" – that is, a spectator who experiences the work with understanding – can see whatever it is in the picture, then it counts as being in the picture. So, to sort out our disagreement, we need to sort out whether a spectator who experiences *Hotel Bedroom* with understanding would, or would not, see the tension in it.

You might find this reliance on reports from a suitable spectator about what can or cannot be seen in the picture a little unsatisfactory. Is there really nothing that can be said about what it is possible to see and what is not possible to see? I am sure I shall never be able to see water as H_2O or my desk as having been manufactured in Dagenham. What I am relying on here is a broad grasp of what could and could not be made visible. Because paintings are concerned with the visible, we can be reasonably sure that there are some things we could not be brought to see in them. After all, I claimed above that we could not see what year the work was painted.

Whether or not we take this as our resting point depends on large issues that I shall not be able to explore in depth. In my discussion, I have assumed that, in working out that content of the work we should talk about our vision and our visual capacities. That much is uncontroversial; however, there is disagreement about how best to construe what we see. I have followed Wollheim in talking of the usual objects of perception: a woman, a hotel room and (possibly) a tense situation. There are some approaches that do not so much take what we see to be objects of perception, but take pictures instead to be made up of symbols within a symbol system. This is clearly correct to an extent. We have already seen that a bowl can be a symbol of female sexuality, to which we can add cats being symbols of fickleness, dogs being symbols of faithfulness, lambs being symbols of innocence and so on. However, the theory I have in mind is stronger than that.

Language is a symbol system. The word "cat" in the sentence "The cat sat on the mat" is a symbol for a certain kind of fluffy animal that goes around the world. There is a long and distinguished tradition in the philosophy of art that holds that there is a symbol system of depiction within which pictures and the elements that go to make up pictures are symbols. The tradition – known variously as semiotics or semiology – goes back at least to C. S. Peirce (1940: ch. 7), although it is most fully worked out by Nelson Goodman (1976). If we add two more elements to the theory, we expand the possible resources for the value of art almost indefinitely.

The first of those two resources is that symbols appear in a hierarchy of representations. A certain configuration of paint on a canvas can symbolize a woman. The way that woman is depicted may in turn symbolize something about her identity: perhaps an honest woman, a courtesan or a prostitute. That in turn can symbolize something else: something perhaps about the position of a person with that identity within a society. The second of the two resources is that such hierarchies of representations are indicative of certain ways of conceiving the world (in short, they are ideological). That is, a picture can be interpreted as a hierarchy of symbols to show how the artist – or the society served by the artist – views the world.

The power of such a conception is demonstrated in a classic study of Manet's painting, *Olympia*, by the art historian T. J. Clark. *Olympia* is ostensibly a painting of a naked woman lounging on a bed, being brought a bouquet of flowers by her servant. As the elements of the painting are symbols, which can themselves be symbols, Clark is able to move fairly quickly from this mundane description to more exotic claims that nakedness signifies class, style signifies ideology and the flatness of the painting (by which he means its flattened perspective, not its literal flatness) signifies modernity (Clark 1985). He is, through this method, able to build almost limitless content into the picture: we see not only a naked woman on a bed, but also class, ideology and modernity. If this is possible, then, even on the theory I favour, the grounds of the value that a picture could have increase enormously. My claim is that the value of a picture is the non-instrumental value of the experience had by someone who understands the picture. If that experience can include the kinds of thing that Clark is talking about, the grounds could be almost limitless.

Whether the grounds of value could be almost limitless depends on whether the view that pictures are hierarchies of symbols is correct. The view has had some very able proponents but, in my view, it cannot be defended. This is neither to deny that some elements of paintings are symbols for some things, nor to deny that paintings can inform us about the circumstances of their production. Instead of going through the various arguments for the view, I shall instead focus on the implausibility of the conclusion. There just seems to be a fundamental difference between words on a page and paintings. We read the first; they are symbols, and the symbols can themselves be symbols. They do not look like the things they are symbols of. It seems forced to say we "read" paintings; we do not, we look at them. What is more, in some way (a way that is surprisingly difficult to make clear) paintings generally look like the things they are paintings of while words do not. Words are symbols within a symbol system but paintings need some other explanation.

Let us sum up where we have got to. The question we started with concerned the value of a work of art. We concluded that whatever the value was, it was not an instrumental value; rather, it was the non-instrumental value of the experience of the work itself. This does not mean any value of any experience: rather, it is the non-instrumental value of the experience of the work that would be had by someone who understands the work. Does this mean that the value of works of art is objective? Well, if "objective" means that the value should be agreed on by everyone then we have looked at reasons for thinking it is not "objective". However, if "objective" only means that the value does not depend on particular individuals on particular occasions, then it is objective. That is, I can be wrong about the value of a work of art; I might think it is bad when in fact it is good, and might think it is good when in fact it is bad.

3. EXPRESSION

Mark Rothko's *Black on Maroon*

In the previous chapter I discussed Mark Rothko's paintings for the Four Seasons Restaurant. To reiterate, in 1958 Rothko was commissioned by the Seagram Company to provide a number of paintings to decorate the restaurant of their new office building in East 52nd Street, New York. One of those paintings, *Black on Maroon*, is the example for study in this chapter on expression. The painting, which dates from 1959, is large: 228.6 cm × 207 cm. It has a dark maroon rectangle painted on a lighter maroon background. On this darker rectangle are two even lighter rectangles, positioned vertically. What are we to make of this painting? What has this painting to do with expression? In answering the first of these questions, it is worth our considering the whole issue of non-figurative art. Once we have done that, we can return to the issue of expression.

In the *Republic*, Plato compares painting to "holding a mirror up to nature" (596d). A painting captures the appearance of a scene or an object, and evaluating that painting is largely a matter of judging how well or badly that appearance has been captured. As we saw in the previous chapter, artistic value is going to involve a more complicated story than that (and it is worth bearing in mind that Plato did not intend his analogy to be flattering) but this characterization will suit our purposes for the moment. Compare paintings that capture an appearance of a scene or object (which I shall call "figurative paintings") with paintings that do not (which I shall call "non-figurative paintings"). If, as I have intimated, the point and value of the first sort of painting is to capture the appearances of scenes or objects, what is the point of the second sort? What could be interesting about two rectangles of lighter paint sitting on top of a larger rectangle of darker paint?

We can see how to answer this question if we take a step back and consider the broader question of the kind of thing a painting – any sort of painting – is. We can approach this by pinpointing the difference between experiencing a painted surface that is not a painting (e.g. an ordinary painted wall) and a painted surface that is a painting. What do we see when we look at a painted wall? The example I am considering is simply a standard painted wall that does not feature anything artistic or interesting. It seems that we simply see it for what it is: a two-dimensional painted surface. What do we see when we look at a picture? Consider, for example, a picture of a bridge with a barn in the background. Once again, we (standardly) see this as a two-dimensional painted surface. We are very rarely deceived into thinking that, instead of being faced with a picture of something, we are faced with a window providing a view of that very thing. However, as well as seeing the picture as a two-dimensional painted surface (or, sometimes, as a three-dimensional surface where the third dimension is only the thickness of the paint) our experience has a different aspect. We look at the painting and say things such as "the barn is behind the bridge". Obviously, a barn cannot be behind a bridge unless the barn and the bridge are positioned relative to each other in *three-dimensional* space. In other words, the difference between a mere painted wall and a picture is that, in the latter, in addition to our being aware of it as a two-dimensional painted surface, we have an experience of a three-dimensional illusory space.

The conception of paintings as objects that provide this distinctive "double-aspect" experience was pioneered by Ernst Gombrich and Richard Wollheim. This approach raises many different questions. What do we say of *trompe l'oeil* paintings: paintings that provide us with the experience of being faced, not by a painting, but by the scene or object itself? Because these do not provide the "double-aspect" experience, are they not really paintings? At the other end of the scale, what about those paintings in which an artist might have applied only the palest of colour washes so that the surface appears to lack the illusion of three dimensions? Once again, one of the aspects of the double-aspect experience would seem to be missing. Even if those problems can be solved, other problems loom. What is the relation between the two aspects of our experience? Do we simply have an experience of a two-dimensional painted surface *and* an experience of three-dimensional illusory space, or are they more intimately related? Finally, what is it to have an experience of three-dimensional illusory space? How similar or different is it from the experience of actual three-dimensional space? These questions have been much debated (Wollheim 1980). The details of these debates need not concern us. All I want to take from this discussion is the point on which most are agreed: that the experience of a picture is, characteristically, an experience of three-dimensional illusory space in a two-dimensional painted surface.

Painters can create the illusion of three dimensions in a variety of ways, such as the use of perspective, chiaroscuro, or simply relations between colours. How they do it is a question for psychology rather than philosophy. The question the painter faces is what to "put into" the three-dimensional space, and in what relations. The important issue for my purposes, which has been underpinning this discussion, is that the significant contrast here is between painted surfaces that do not provide an experience of illusory depth (such as ordinary painted walls) and painted surfaces that do provide such an experience (pictures). Within the latter category the artist will need to decide whether the three dimensions should "contain" (to find a way of putting it) "objects that can be met with in space", such as bridges and barns, or "contain" abstract shapes and solids. In other words, the distinction between figurative and non-figurative paintings is not the significant distinction; it is a distinction within paintings. Why I describe this as "not the significant distinction" is that what figurative and non-figurative paintings have in common (namely, the double aspect to the experience) is more important than what they do not have in common (namely, that in one case what populates the illusory space are things such as bridges and barns, and in the other case not) (Wollheim 1987: 62).

A reproduction of a work seldom provides an experience equivalent to looking at the work. This is particularly so in the case of Rothko. The photograph reproduced here in the plate section is 16.6 cm × 11.7 cm. *Black on Maroon* is 228.6 cm × 207 cm. That is, it is a large painting that provides a rather overwhelming visual experience (which is not yet to say anything about the value of that experience). The first question to ask, then, is what we see when we look at *Black on Maroon*. One possibility is that we do not see it as a picture at all. Rather, like the painted wall, we simply see it as a two-dimensional painted surface. However, this is not the experience the canvas prompts. What many people find surprising about Rothko's work is the depth of the pictorial space he manages to achieve. The dark colours seem take us way back into pictorial space. This provides at least the initial answer to the question posed earlier as to what could be interesting about a painting of rectangles. What is interesting about it is what is interesting about any painting: it provides the "double-aspect" experience – an experience of three dimensions in a two-dimensional painted surface.

Of course, this is only the beginning of the story. An experience of rectangles related in pictorial space would not in itself appear to be particularly valuable. What do we see when we look at the picture? The picture gives rise to different experiences. You can see the two lighter rectangles as being in the foreground, like pillars seen against a darker background. Alternatively, you can see them as a light background perceived through a darker wall. While executing the Seagram commission, Rothko changed from using primarily horizontal bands of colour to using vertical bands, which has prompted one commentator to remark: "While still predominantly rectangular, this new imagery, suggesting windows, doors, portals, was simple, classical, architectural" (Breslin 1993: 382–3). The suggestiveness of Rothko's imagery is captured in a celebrated paragraph by the art critic David Sylvester:

> The … emphatic frontality of a Rothko creates a related kind of confrontation. Here we are faced with a highly ambiguous presence which seems, on the one hand, ethereal, empty, on the other solid and imposing, like a megalith. It is a presence that alternates between seeming to be receptive, intimate, enveloping, and seeming to be menacing, repelling. It plays with us as the weather does, for it is a landscape, looming up over us, evoking the elements, recalling the imagery of the first verses of the Book of Genesis – the darkness upon the face of the deep, the dividing of the light from the darkness, the creation of the firmament, the dividing of the waters from the waters. "Often, towards nightfall", Rothko once said to me, "there is a feeling in the air of mystery, threat, frustration – all of these at once. I would like my painting to have the quality of such moments." And, of course, it does have that quality; it belongs to the great Romantic tradition of the sublime landscape.   (Sylvester 1996: 327)

We can divide what Sylvester finds in a Rothko into two kinds of property. On the one hand he sees three-dimensional shapes: whether megaliths or the dividing of the waters (to which we can add, for the more prosaic of us, windows, doors and portals). On the other hand, he does not see things in the painting, but instead detects the presence of emotions: intimacy, menace, mystery, threat and frustration. For the remainder of this chapter, we are going to look at this: the relation between a picture and the emotions. In particular, we shall attempt to throw light on the *expression* of emotion by a picture.

As ever in thinking deeply about anything, it is important to know exactly what the question is for which we are looking for an answer. According to

Sylvester, it is apt to characterize Rothko's pictures using words such as "intimacy", "menace", "mystery", "threat" and "frustration". Somehow, the fact that these words seem apt presents a problem; what we need to sort out is what exactly that problem is. Here are two possible issues that might be bothering us, and it is important to distinguish between them.

The first possible problem concerns *why* we come to experience the pictures in a way that makes it apt for us to describe them in those terms. Consider a non-artistic context in which it might be apt to describe something in terms of threat: say, we are faced with a snarling dog. If we ask what it is about the situation that causes us to describe it in this way, we might refer to the growl, the sharp teeth, the imminent danger and so on. That is, we find features of the situation that explain why we come to have the experience that we do. What are the features of the Rothko that explain why "threat" is the apt word to use? All we are faced with are some painted shapes that are not dangerous and hence not a threat to anyone. What features of the painting cause us to describe the painting in terms of threat?

This is the same kind of question one might ask about arachnophobia. Some people seem terrified of spiders, which, they are quite willing to admit, are harmless and hence no threat at all. Attempts have been made (although apparently without much success) to identify the features of the spider that cause such a reaction. What is interesting is the kind of people doing such an investigation: scientists. That is, to discover what it is about spiders that prompts such terror we need to do some empirical work, whether in cross-cultural comparisons, or evolutionary psychology or sociology. It is not obvious the philosopher has much to contribute: you are not going to be able to find out what features of the spider cause terror from your armchair. It is the same situation with the Rothko. We can speculate on what features of the Rothko cause us to describe it by the word "threat". It might be something to do with the depth of colour, or with the effect of one rectangle floating on another in illusory space, or with something else. Unless we do the hard empirical work of comparative analysis of various different pictures, we are not going to find out for certain. That is, to summarize, the *mechanism* by which we come to describe the picture in the way we do is a matter for science (in particular, psychology) and not a matter for philosophy.

Having put the first issue aside, what of the second issue? Let us go back to the snarling dog and the aptness of describing the dog in terms of a threat. What makes it apt? Here the answer is easy: the object of the person's fear (what they are afraid of) is something it makes perfect sense to be afraid of: a snarling dog. It makes perfect sense because the fact that the dog is snarling probably means it is angry, and angry dogs are prone to bite, and being bitten by a dog is painful and probably injurious. Hence, when the person claims that the dog is a threat this does not raise any difficult issues; it is all too obvious what they are trying to communicate to us. In the case of the Rothko, it is not so clear. What exactly is Sylvester trying to say when he says (or Rothko says) that the paintings have an air of threat? The claim lacks a context in which it makes any sense. Paintings do not bite and the visual experience of paintings is not injurious. What sense does it make to claim that it is apt to describe some painted rectangles as having an air of threat? To describe the experience as being of a coloured surface, of rectangles, or of a painting, makes perfect sense; there is no mystery as to what someone would be trying to communicate. But to describe the experience as one that "alternates between seeming to be receptive, intimate, enveloping, and seeming to be menacing, repelling" (to shift to another part of Sylvester's description) does raise the question of what it is the critic is trying to communicate. Hence, the philosophical issue is to attempt to throw light on what is being communicated. We have a sense of what it is (we do not take Sylvester simply to be talking nonsense). Can we articulate this sense and make it more precise?

I am going to consider three replies that might occur to you. The first is arousalism: a painting can be aptly described using a certain emotional term if that is how it makes its viewers feel. If people feel something like threat when faced with Rothko's painting (whatever the mechanism for causing such a feeling) then it is apt to describe the painting in terms of threat. If it makes them feel restful, it is apt to describe the painting as restful. Generalizing, we can say that, for any emotion E:

> A painting can aptly be described in terms of E if and only if it makes any of its viewers feel E.

We should make one alteration before considering this theory. We need to put some restriction on which viewers' reactions count. If we say "any of its viewers", the painting might end up being described in ways we do not think are right. We can borrow one important restriction from Chapter 2, and limit ourselves to viewers who understand the painting. After all, it would not be right to describe a gripping game of cricket as boring simply because it bored one of the spectators who did not understand it. However, that will not solve the problem altogether, as some skewed reactions are not a matter of a failure of understanding. What of weird viewers, who feel (say) angry whenever they see red? Even the most tranquil painting that features a red patch will make them angry. If they are viewers who understand the picture, that would mean that those paintings would be aptly described as angry, which, again, does not seem right. It may be impossible to specify, in a non-circular manner, a "standard" viewer: one who has the right kinds of reactions. However, as the theory suffers from an even greater problem, let us put a place-holder in for the moment.

> A painting can aptly be described in terms of E if and only if it makes a standard viewer, whose reactions are grounded in understanding the painting, feel E.

One advantage with this theory is that it uses something we have anyway: our reactions to a painting. Viewers report a range of emotional reactions to Rothko's works, generally of the sort Sylvester describes. The theory, however, has a serious flaw. Let us look again at the claims Sylvester makes. First, he says: "Here *we are faced* with a highly ambiguous presence which seems, on the one hand, ethereal, empty, on the other solid and imposing, like a megalith. *It is a presence* that alternates between seeming to be receptive, intimate, enveloping, and seeming to be menacing, repelling." Second, he agrees with Rothko that "there is a feeling in the air of mystery, threat, frustration – all of these at once. I would like *my painting* to have the quality of such moments." Notice the words that I have italicized. The claim by both men is that something we are faced with, some presence, some painting, has the qualities under discussion. That is, we are talking about features *out there*: something we see *in the painting*. Arousalism, by contrast, talks about a feeling that is *in the viewer*. If we follow arousalism, the feature ends up in the wrong place. It equates seeing threat in a painting with seeing a painting and feeling threatened. However, the second is simply not the right way to describe the first. The first describes *a way of experiencing the painting*; the second simply describes something felt by the viewer. The fact that arousalism does not answer the question we are trying to answer does not mean that we have to give up the claim that pictures arouse our feelings. They frequently do. The issue is whether these aroused feelings can account for our describing *the pictures* in terms such as "menace", "mystery", "threat" and "frustration". It seems that it cannot.

The second reply to the question does not focus on how the viewer feels but (rather more appropriately) on how the painting looks. Instead of (for example) a sad painting being one that makes us feel sad, a sad painting is one that looks like a sad person. This might appear to be an answer to the wrong question: that is, to the psychological question identified above. It appears as if what it is saying is that the feature that causes us to describe the painting as "sad" is its resemblance to a sad person. This may, for all I know, be correct: resemblance may be the mechanism by which we come to experience the painting as sad. That, as I said above, is something that would need to be sorted out by empirical investigation. However, it is also an answer to the philosophical question: the attempt to throw light on what someone who describes a picture in terms such as "sad" is trying to say. What they are trying to say, according to this account, is that it looks like a sad person or, more formally, that they experience it as being similar to a sad person. This account has an advantage over arousalism in that it gets the emotion in the right place: in the painting. Putting the same restriction in place as we did for arousalism, the account is as follows:

> A painting can aptly be described in terms of E if and only if a standard viewer, whose reactions are grounded in understanding the painting, experiences the painting as resembling a person expressing (or in some other way manifesting) E.

The account, however, suffers from one obvious drawback. Looking back at Sylvester's description, the account claims that we would experience *Black on Maroon* as resembling a person manifesting at least some of intimacy, menace, threat and frustration. However, we do not experience it in this way. We might indeed experience it as resembling megaliths or the dividing of the waters, but (to put matters bluntly) there are countless paintings including this one that are apt to be described in emotion terms that look nothing like a person expressing (or in some other way manifesting) that emotion.

What are perhaps the obvious accounts (a sad painting is one that makes us sad, and a sad painting is one that looks like a sad person) are not the answer to our question. This is not to deny that some sad paintings do make us sad and some sad paintings do resemble sad people. It is only that the accounts do not provide a *general* answer to the question of what someone is trying to communicate in describing a painting in terms usually reserved for the emotions. For the moment let us continue to attempt to find a general answer; we shall consider the wisdom of doing so below.

In his book *Sight and Sensibility*, Dominic Lopes has made some helpful distinctions (the rest of this discussion is greatly indebted to Lopes). First, consider a painting of a person who is manifesting some emotion, for example Frans Hals's painting *The Jolly Drinker* (c. 1628). This depicts a jolly fellow, and the painting is itself aptly described as jolly. The jollity of the painting is attributable to the jollity of the figure depicted in it. This, Lopes describes as "figure expression": "an expression that is wholly attributable to the depicted person or persons" (Lopes 2005: 51). Second, there are paintings that do not depict figures that manifest a certain emotion, but depict scenes that are aptly described using emotion terms. Consider the aptly named *The Gloomy Day*, by Pieter Breughel (1565). This depicts a rather bleak winter landscape, with a gathering storm. The figures in it are not themselves gloomy; they are busily preparing for the harsh months ahead. However, the painting is aptly described as gloomy: a gloomy painting that is not of gloomy people. This Lopes calls "scene expression": "an expression that is attributable at least in part to a depicted scene and is not wholly attributable to any depicted persons" (*ibid.*: 52).

Only paintings that depict things in the world (whether figures or scenes) can exhibit figure expression or scene expression. However, *Black on Maroon* does neither: it is a non-figurative painting. Whatever expression it has is attributable directly to the painting's design. Hence, Lopes introduces a third category of expression, "design expression": "an expression that is wholly attributable to a picture's design or surface and not to any figure or scene it depicts" (*ibid.*: 57).

It might seem that the purpose of these distinctions is to separate the unproblematic cases of expression (figure expression and scene expression) from the problematic case (design expression). The former pair are unproblematic because when we say that Frans Hals's painting is jolly or Pieter Breughel's painting is gloomy what we are really saying is that the pictures depict someone who would look jolly if seen face to face and a landscape that would look gloomy if seen face to face. What someone who describes a painting using emotion terms is trying to convey, in these instances, is simply that the painting depicts something (a figure or scene) to which those terms would apply if we saw what is depicted face to face.

However, as Lopes points out, such optimism would be misplaced. Let us consider figure expression first. Most would agree that Edvard Munch's *The Scream* (1893) expresses existential angst. Let us say that this angst is wholly attributable to the figure in the foreground. However, were you to encounter that figure face to face they would not be expressing existential angst. I doubt they would be expressing anything at all; they would look too weird (nobody you might meet in the world looks like the figure in Munch's painting). Lopes gives a nice example of an *Asterix* book, *La Zizanie*, in which the Gauls succumb to a contagion of anger (Lopes attributes this to Forceville [2005]).

> Anger is shown by multiple superimpositions of an angry figure or by separating it from the ground plane, as if shaking; by spiral lines fanning out from the figure's head; by straight lines radiating from the mouth, as if expelling something with great force; and by smoke emanating from the angry figure's head.   (Lopes 2005: 80)

The conclusion to draw from this is that painters (or cartoonists) have more tricks up their sleeve in presenting us with figures that manifest a certain emotion than simply painting how a person manifesting that emotion would look face to face. Indeed, simply painting how a person manifesting that emotion would look face to face sometimes results in a figure that looks weird, in the way that a still photograph of someone shouting or crying sometimes looks weird. So what someone is trying to communicate when they describe a picture in terms usually reserved for the emotions, and the expression is wholly attributable to the depicted figure, is not that these are the emotion terms it would be appropriate to use were we to see the figure face to face. Even with figure expression, our problem is still unresolved.

The same issue arises with scene expression. There are instances of scene expression in art where what is depicted could not be seen face to face; the scene is depicted in a way that is artistically *sui generis*. Van Gogh's *Wheatfield with Crows* (1890) is an instance of this. The emotional darkness of the painting is a case of scene expression. However, if you were to see the field as it was in the world, it would not have the same emotional darkness; it would, like Munch's figure, just look weird. Of course, you would not be able to see the field as van Gogh painted it in the world; no such field exists, or ever has existed.

There is an additional reason for thinking our optimism about scene expression is misplaced. We can, unproblematically, use emotion terms to describe people seen face to face. Indeed, this is their central use. The reason it is their central use is that what we mean when we say someone *is* jolly (or sad, or jealous) is that they *feel* jolly (or sad, or jealous). Were we to meet the jolly drinker face to face, we could describe him as jolly because he feels jolly. It is less obvious what we are trying to say when use emotion terms to describe scenes seen face to face. In describing a landscape as "gloomy" or "harrowing" we clearly do not mean that they *feel* gloomy or harrowing (being insensate, they do not feel anything). Thus, describing a landscape as "gloomy" or "harrowing" seems to raise the same problem as describing a picture as "gloomy" or "harrowing". What would someone who described a landscape in those terms be trying to communicate? It would be wrong to claim that scene expression is not a problem because all we are trying to say is what we would be trying to say if we saw the scene face to face. It would be wrong because we do not know what we would be trying to say if we used these terms to describe the scene face to face.

We do not yet have the answer to our philosophical problem. Even in cases of figure and scene expression, the person who describes a painting in terms usually reserved for the emotions does not mean what he or she would mean were he or she to see what is depicted face to face. Furthermore, the account could not even aspire to answer the question with respect to design expression where there is nothing that *could* be seen face to face.

The third and final reply to the question is similar to the one we have just considered except that it does not focus on the painting looking like someone or something expressing (or in some other way manifesting) an emotion. Instead, it draws on the viewer's imagination (what follows is a reconstruction of a view somewhat like that of Bruce Vermazen [1986]). Let us start with what we mean by "expression" in the everyday sense. It will be something like this: someone is expressing an emotion if they are manifesting some appearance or behaviour that is evidence that they are feeling that emotion. For example, you express your happiness by laughing, for laughing is evidence that you feel happy. We apply this literally to works of art. That is, works of art express an emotion if they are evidence that the maker felt that emotion. There is one clarification that needs to be made before we can assess the view: who exactly is "the maker". It could be the actual maker. This leads to all kinds of problems, however. For example, excessively sentimental paintings of large-eyed young girls weeping over broken toys are fairly clear evidence that the actual maker is not feeling any emotion (except perhaps a slight cynicism). Instead, we should consider a hypothetical maker: a persona. That is, we disregard the actual maker and instead ask ourselves something like the following question: assuming whoever it was that made this painting were successful in expressing their emotion in the painting, what emotion would they be expressing? (We shall come back to the contrast between the actual and the hypothetical maker in Chapter 5.) More formally, we might put it as follows:

A painting expresses an emotion E if and only if attributing E to the (hypothetical) maker of the object would explain the painting's having the features it has.

Sylvester would be right in attributing menace to Rothko's painting only if that would explain the painting having the features it has: the particular set of colour and spatial arrangements we find in the pictorial space of that painting.

One advantage with this view is that it is completely general: it accounts for my laughing being an expression of my happiness, and the look of Rothko's painting being an expression of menace and threat. However, there is an obvious problem. Laughing is evidence that someone feels happy because laughing is what people produce when they are happy, yet it is simply not the case (it is nowhere near the case) that being a set of rectangles related in a particular way in pictorial space is what people produce when they are menacing. Clearly, something needs to be added to the view.

What is added is something like this. The painting is such as to cause the standard viewer to imagine of the work that it is evidence of the feeling of menace by its (hypothetical) maker. Obviously, the work is not evidence of the feeling of menace by anyone, real or hypothetical, any more than two sticks tied together is a sword. However, it can be imagined to be evidence of the feeling of menace in the same way as two sticks can be imagined to be a sword. Putting in the emendation leaves us with this:

> A painting expresses an emotion E if and only if it causes the standard viewer to imagine that attributing E to the (hypothetical) maker of the object would explain the painting's having the features it has.

This demands quite a stretch. I can understand what it is to imagine of two pieces of wood that are tied together that they are a sword: the sticks of wood and the sword have a great deal in common that make that act of imagining easy. The contrast with Rothko's painting is stark. The whole problem is that they do not have anything in common with that which people produce when they feel an emotion; if they did there would be no problem. It is simply not clear what we are being asked to do when we are asked to imagine of Rothko's rectangles that they are evidence of menace. Let us simplify matters and hold that, in the central case, menace is expressed either through the voice (shouting) or through behaviour (waving one's arms, threateningly). Are we being asked to imagine of Rothko's rectangles that they are shouting or waving one's arms about? That does not seem feasible. The alternative is that we are being asked to imagine that, in addition to shouting and waving one's arms about, human beings have another way of expressing menace: namely, the spontaneous production of rectangles of the sort that Rothko has produced. However, this seems bizarre; we surely cannot be being asked to imagine that. As neither alternative seems satisfactory, I am not sure how our third reply could be completed. (This discussion has drawn on a much neglected discussion by Malcolm Budd of theories of expression that involve the imagination; see Budd 1985: 133–44.)

As we saw in Chapter 1 in our attempt to define "art", it is a good rule of thumb in philosophy that when an attempt to find an answer grinds to a halt, go back and review the question. It might be that, instead of there being an answer out there that we are failing to find, there is no answer to the question as posed; we have asked the wrong question. This is the case here. I have been asking: what is someone who describes a picture using terms that usually refer to the emotions trying to communicate? We have considered various answers, and found that they could not be generally true. It is not true of all pictures described as sad that they arouse sadness in a viewer or resemble a sad person, nor that their contents would look sad seen face to face. However, each of these could be what someone who described some particular picture as sad was trying to communicate. Budd has put the point as follows: "the content or point of a purely descriptive aesthetic judgement is rarely manifest in the judgement's linguistic expression" (2008b: 77). In other words, what someone is trying to communicate in describing a picture using terms that usually refer to the emotions may vary from case to case, even if they use the very same words on each occasion.

To see this, let us contrast Georges de la Tour's *St Joseph* (1642) with the example we are considering in this chapter. *St Joseph* is a dark painting, depicting the inside of Joseph's carpentry workshop. Joseph, an old man, is working a piece of wood while being lectured to by the young Jesus, illuminated by the candle he holds. The augur Joseph is turning into a beam is parallel to the picture plane, giving a clear symbol of the cross. What one would be attempting to communicate in describing the picture as "sad" (which would be a prosaic description, but we have to start somewhere) may well be something to do with the irony of the painting. What it depicts could not be more innocent: a beautiful child talking to his father, who works in an honest trade. Counterposed to this is our knowledge of the future of the child, the echo of the cross, the troubled look on Joseph's face, the hint – on Jesus's face – that he knows his fate, and the contrast between the light and the dark. In calling this picture "sad" we would be gesturing to features such as these. If somebody asks what we mean, it is features such as these that we will cite.

Sylvester is not alone in describing Rothko's work in terms of the negative emotions. Wollheim described another of the Four Season's series, *Red on Maroon*, as expressing "a form of suffering and of sorrow … somehow barely or fragilely contained" (Wollheim 1973b: 128). What are Wollheim (and Sylvester, when he is using emotion terms) trying to communicate? They are clearly not drawing on the narrative content of the picture (as we were with *St Joseph*) as there is no narrative content. Hence, what is being communicated when it is said of *St Joseph* that it is melancholy will almost certainly not be what is being communicated when it is said of *Black on Maroon* that it is melancholy. Hence, the question as I framed it – What, in general, would someone be trying to communicate who described a painting in terms more usually reserved for the emotions? – is ill formed. If the critic is trying to communicate different things on different occasions, then it does not look as if there is much we can usefully contribute on a general level. Whether or not an emotion term applies in a particular case is a matter best left to art critics, rather than philosophers (Budd 2008a: 152).

What, then, should we say about our example, Rothko's *Black on Maroon*? What does Sylvester mean when he says that "[i]t is a presence that alternates between seeming to be receptive, intimate, enveloping, and seeming to be menacing, repelling"? He does go on immediately to enlarge upon his claim:

> It plays with us as the weather does, for it is a landscape, looming up
> over us, evoking the elements, recalling the imagery of the first verses
> of the Book of Genesis – the darkness upon the face of the deep, the
> dividing of the light from the darkness, the creation of the firmament,
> the dividing of the waters from the waters.   (Sylvester 1996: 327)

What Sylvester is trying to say (or, at least, a gesture towards what he is trying to say) is that we should look at Rothko's paintings as we might (for example) sometimes look at the night sky. When we look at the night sky we look into something the size of which is beyond our comprehension, and the nature of which is beyond our understanding: something that contains innumerable planets, of which an innumerable number might contain civilizations something like ours, which will undergo the cycle of birth, life and death and of which we will never know anything. (I have borrowed this description from Budd, who in turn borrows it from Kant.) We should not see the painting as a depiction of rectangles as portals and windows, but we should rather see it as a depiction of something beyond comprehension and understanding: "the dividing of the light from the darkness, the creation of the firmament, the dividing of the waters from the waters". This can comfort us (we are part of it) and menace us (we are an insignificant part of an insignificant part of it). What does the painting express? The awe and terror of something too vast for us to comprehend, yet which can comfort us as we cannot, now, be destroyed by it. In other words, as Sylvester goes on to say, it belongs in the tradition of paintings of nature at its most magnificent and moody: paintings by, for example, Turner, Constable and Friedrich.

In one sense, then, the conclusion is rather disappointing. Philosophy cannot throw much light on what critics are trying to communicate when they describe paintings in terms usually reserved for the emotions, because philosophy deals in general truths and what is being communicated depends on the particular painting being talked about and possibly even the particular context of utterance. However, philosophy embraces both a negative and a positive project; it can sometimes be as valuable to point out where we have gone wrong as it can be to show us how to go right. In this area, the negative project has proved most useful; the question of what a critic is trying to communicate in describing a painting in terms more usually reserved for the emotions is not a good question. There is no one thing such a judgement is trying to communicate; what the critic is trying to say will vary with painting and with circumstance. The critic could be drawing attention to the effect of the work, to resemblances between the work and the manifestation of a particular emotion, to whatever it is the work depicts, or could be saying something else (Budd 2008b). The critic might even find it difficult to characterize what he or she is saying in other terms, or to provide reasons why what he or she is saying is appropriate. However, once what is being discussed is whether particular features of particular works justify particular judgements, it is time for the philosopher to bow out and leave matters to the critic.

4. FORGERIES, COPIES AND VARIATIONS

Gerhard Richter's *Dead 2*

Forgeries, copies and variations encompass a whole range of interesting problems within the arts. Indeed, we can add homages and quotations to the mix of different issues that flourish in the same hedgerow. Unlike the other chapters in this book, I shall not start by discussing a case study. That is because the case study, Gerhard Richter's *Dead 2*, is a copy, albeit of a complex kind, and the most enlightening place to begin is somewhere else: with forgeries.

A forger of paintings can do one of two things. First, he or she could forge an existing painting and attempt to pass it off as that particular painting. Second, he or she could produce a painting and attempt, fraudulently, to pass it off as being by someone else. The first might seem a rather daft endeavour because we usually know the whereabouts of existing paintings. You would need to be rather dim-witted to try to sell a forgery of the *Mona Lisa* given that it is well known that the *Mona Lisa* is hanging in the Louvre. However, it is not hard to think of circumstances in which it might be sensible to create a copy of the *Mona Lisa* and try to sell it. Imagine the *Mona Lisa* was stolen and its whereabouts were unknown. It might then be worth trying to convince some rich and unscrupulous collector to add "the *Mona Lisa*" to his or her private collection. Perhaps more plausibly, we might know of some painting that is lost. Many well-documented works of art in Russia and Europe disappeared during the Second World War and an enterprising forger might "discover" one of them in an obscure attic and try to reintroduce it (at great expense, no doubt) to the art world.

This first kind of forgery is wrong because it is deceitful. That is not the particularly interesting issue for us, however. The more interesting issue is the value of the forgery as a painting; is it worse as a painting for being a copy of another painting? What is the relative value of the original and the forgery, and why? I shall discuss this when I come to talk about copies. Before that, however, there is the second and more interesting kind of forgery to consider.

In a career that lasted over ten years, the Dutch forger Han van Meegeren painted a number of works that he passed off as the works of some great painters of the past. The pinnacle of his career was a forged Vermeer, *The Supper at Emmaus* (1937). There are a number of fascinating aspects to van Meegeren's career, which raise a number of interesting questions. Of these, the most philosophically relevant is whether being a forgery makes a difference to the painting as a painting. Idealizing the story somewhat, van Meegeren painted the picture and persuaded the principal expert on Vermeer to authenticate it. It was bought for a huge sum of money and donated to a museum in Rotterdam where it was much admired. When the deception was revealed (in 1945) the painting – now worth considerably less – was removed from its place on the wall. Our question is whether this was justified: is the painting worth less *as a painting* once it is discovered that people were mistaken about who painted it?

It is easy to construct the case as to why being a forgery should *not* make a difference. Let us draw on the view expressed in Chapter 2: that the value of a painting is something to do with how it *looks*. *Supper at Emmaus*, let us suppose, did not *look* different once people had discovered it was by not by Vermeer but by van Meegeren. It did not look different so how can its value be different? The only difference is that the observers changed from believing it was by Vermeer to believing it was by van Meegeren. However, the very same painting was in front of them. The value of the painting is the non-instrumental value of the experience they have of the painting (provided they understand the painting). If they thought it was wonderful beforehand, what could justify them changing their mind? Indeed, one could go so far (as Alfred Lessing has) as to think that such a change of mind is evidence of snobbery (Lessing 1965).

One reply to this charge of snobbery is to take the heroic line of agreeing with the argument that the value of a painting depends only on how it looks, but denying the conclusion. That is, the heroic line maintains that *Supper at Emmaus* never looked good in the first place. It was never, in fact, a good painting. If one does maintain this line, however, one needs to explain why people in 1937 *thought* it was a good painting. After all, the people in 1937 (some of whom, as we have seen, were Vermeer experts) had the same access to the painting as we do. Here some facts about human psychology could come to the heroic line's rescue. For a start, people at the time were very keen to find another Vermeer (particularly a Vermeer that dealt with a reli-gious subject matter) and if people want something badly enough then they are less likely to question it when it is given to them. Second, the principal expert had authenticated it; for others to disagree would be to risk ridicule (this does not, of course, explain how the principal expert was fooled). Third, and perhaps most intriguingly, people are often blind to stylistic features of their own age. You need only recall looking at photographs of yourself from ten or twenty years ago. Those clothes of which you were so proud, which looked so natural at the time you barely noticed their style, now scream out at you as exemplars of the decade during with the photograph was taken. A photograph that was taken during the 1980s looks as if it was taken dur-ing the 1980s. According to Denis Dutton, the same is true of *The Supper at Emmaus*. If we look at the painting now, it has some of the features of images popular in the 1930s. Dutton claims the faces are strongly influenced by con-temporary cinema photographs; indeed, he even claims that one of the faces displays a striking resemblance to Greta Garbo (Dutton 2003: 262). Thus, the reason people in 1937 thought it was a good painting is because they were blind to certain features, features that, when they start to become visible to us, mar the painting. Hence, the heroic line maintains that the painting never was particularly valuable as a painting; it is just that people, encouraged by the thought that it was by Vermeer, mistakenly thought it a good painting.

The heroic line works only if, in fact, people are mistaken in their judge-ment. What if they are not? What if, for example, a forger actually produces a finer painting than many in the *oeuvre* of the artist who, it is claimed, painted it? This would appear possible; after all, everybody (even a great art-ist) is entitled to have an off day. If the forgery is in fact a fine painting, are we forced to the conclusion that it adds value to the world? One argument for thinking not asks us to focus not only on the work by itself, but on the effects it has on our understanding. A forgery – even a fine forgery – does not simply add to the sum of fine things in the world. It affects the way we think about other paintings. Hence, an argument as to why a forgery is not valuable, even if it is a fine painting, is that it distorts our view of the artist. There are thought to be around thirty-five paintings by Vermeer in existence. The discovery of another painting, particularly a major one, would have a profound effect on how we view Vermeer's paintings generally. *The Supper at Emmaus* has certain stylistic features (slightly hooded eyes, rather geometri-cal faces) that authentic works by Vermeer lack. If we took van Meegeren's painting to be genuine, we would start to *see* the others of Vermeer's paint-ings as lacking those features. Indeed, this is what happened. Once *The*

Supper at Emmaus was taken to be genuine, it was easier for van Meegeren to have other paintings accepted as genuine. For those other paintings possessed certain of van Meegeren's stylistic features, which, because they also appeared in *The Supper at Emmaus*, were taken as evidence that the painting was by Vermeer. Of course, it follows from this that what was taken to be a genuine understanding of those pictures was not a genuine understanding at all. Because the value of the pictures is the non-instrumental value of the experience that is had with understanding, the critics' access to the true value of all works by Vermeer was denied.

There is much to be said for the argument that forgeries are bad because they make a genuine understanding of the *oeuvre* of an artist impossible. The problem, however, is even worse than a forgery putting a barrier between the critic and an understanding of an artist's work. A further problem is that, if you are deceived by the forgery, you are condemned to not understanding the work itself. Dutton has identified an element in our understanding of a work that is blocked when we are (unknowingly) faced with a forgery.

Dutton claims that "every work of art ... involves the element of performance" (2002: 102). To illuminate this claim, Dutton gives us an example:

> Consider for a moment Smith and Jones, who have just finished listening to a new recording of Liszt's *Transcendental Études*. Smith is transfixed. He says, "What beautiful artistry! The pianist's tone is superb, his control absolute, his speed and accuracy dazzling. Truly an electric performance!" Jones responds with a sigh. "Yeah, it was electric alright. Or to be more precise, it was electronic. He recorded the music at practice tempo and the engineers speeded it up."
>
> (*Ibid.*: 101)

The point here is that judging the performance is, in part, judging the achievement of the performer. The reason for Smith's enthusiasm was bound up with him judging the achievement of playing at a quick tempo without losing such properties as tone, control and accuracy. Once it is revealed that there was no such achievement, the bottom is knocked out of the judgement. Smith's judgement was wholly inappropriate for the object he was judging.

Even if one grants this in the case of music, what reason is there to think it applies equally to painting? First, we could simply return the question: what reason is there to think it does not apply? What the example shows is that understanding a piece of music is not simply a matter of appreciating how it sounds to an uninformed perceiver. If that is so, why should we think that appreciating a painting is simply a matter of how it looks to an uninformed perceiver? There might be an answer to this: performing a piece of music is a matter of overcoming certain technical difficulties, and part of our judgement of a piece of music is judging how well or badly these difficulties have been overcome. The same does not apply to paintings. However, as Dutton points out, this is incorrect; the same *does* apply to paintings (and does generally across the arts).

> It may be perfectly true (and not necessarily obviously so) to remark that in a painting of the Madonna the pale pink of the Virgin's robe contrasts pleasantly with the light blue-gray of her cloak. But it is far from irrelevant to know that the artist may be working within a canon (as, for example, fifteenth-century Italian artists did) according to which the robe must be some shade of red, and the cloak must be blue. The demand, to juxtapose fundamentally warm and cool colors, poses difficulties for creating harmony between robe and cloak, in the face of which Ghirlandaio may reduce the size of the cloak and tone it down with gray, Perugino may depict the cloak thrown over the Virgin's knees and allow a green shawl with red and yellow stripes to dominate the composition, while Filippo Lippi may simply cover the robe completely with the cloak. To say that the resulting assemblage of colors is pleasant may, again, be true enough; a fuller appreciation and understanding, however, would involve recognizing how that pleasing harmony is a response to a problematic demand put upon the artist. *(Ibid.: 104)*

Dutton has given us an example of a difficulty and three ways in which three great painters overcame that difficulty. If we are faced (unknowingly) with a forgery, part of our judgement will be how whoever we take the painter to be overcame the technical problems that beset those working at the time and in the tradition in which he or she painted. However, those were not the difficulties involved in the production of this particular painting; the difficulties involved in the production of this particular painting were, in the main, how to get it to look like (say) a Vermeer. It is as if we are judging the pianist when really we should be judging the sound engineer. The problem with forgeries is that they misrepresent achievement and, as our judgements on a painting are in part judgements about achievement, our judgements are wholly inappropriate for the objects that we are judging.

71

Dutton, as we have seen, holds that when we judge a painting we are, in part, judging the achievement of the artist. Dutton's view is that different paintings can manifest different achievements: a Vermeer manifests certain achievements by Vermeer, and a van Meegeren manifests certain achievements by van Meegeren. Provided we are not mistaken about the achievements we are judging, our judgements will not fall down (at least, not for that reason). We can judge a painting that is a forgery, provided we judge it as a painting that is a forgery (*ibid.*: 106). Wollheim, however, thinks that to count as a "proper" painting (i.e. one that is worthy of our consideration as a painting), that object has to manifest an achievement of a particular sort: the clarification of an expression of a certain range of mental states by the artist (Wollheim 1994a: 11). Anything that does not do this may look like a painting, but is not a painting (i.e. it is by a "nonpainter").

> [W]hen that judgment that a painting is by a nonpainter rather than by a painter legitimately affects the judgment of quality, it does so, characteristically, not by raising or lowering that judgment, but by knocking it sideways. We lose all confidence in our power to make it. Learning that a painting, believed to be by a painter, is by a non-painter, we are likely to feel that we don't know what to make of, and what weight to attach to, whatever shows up on the painted support. (Wollheim 1994b: 174)

A forger, of course, produces a forgery by painting it. Furthermore, van Meegeren could certainly paint. Wollheim's point is that painting is more than simply putting pigment on canvas; it is doing that with a certain aim, governed by a certain set of motivations. Furthermore, when we look at the painting we see it as being governed by these motivations. When people mistakenly saw van Meegeren's painting as Vermeer's painting, they mistakenly saw the marks as being governed by Vermeer's motivations. However, once they truly understood the painting (i.e. once they discovered that it was painted by van Meegeren) they could not see it like this. As Wollheim says, their judgement was "knocked sideways". It might help to consider an analogy. Imagine overhearing someone describe their feelings following the death of a loved one. You are moved by what seems to you an honest and unsentimental facing-up to what seems unbearable pain. You can hear the regret and anxiety about the future in the phrasing and the tone of voice. Then the voice suddenly says, "Right, I will take it again from the top" and you realize it is an actor practising a speech. In one way nothing has changed (as *The Supper at Emmaus* did not change) but in another way everything has changed. You cannot evaluate what you have heard as someone triumphing over life's misfortunes but can only evaluate it as a copy of someone triumphing over life's misfortunes, however good a copy that might be.

The problems with forgeries revolve around the problems of deception. The work is a fraudulent object; it is masquerading as something it is not. This, as we have seen, leads to a debasement of our understanding of the purported artist and at best a false experience of the work. I propose to leave the discussion of forgeries now and focus instead on a different problem: the problem that arises from copies made without an intention to deceive. These, I think, are even more perplexing. To see why, let us grant the existence of a "super Xerox machine" (Currie 1989). This machine will make an atom-for-atom replica of an existing work of art. Obviously, this will only be able to make copies of existing works of art rather than create new pieces in the style of an artist. Our question is whether the copy would be any less valuable as a work of art than the original.

We can dramatize the question by considering the position of an art gallery in a city far away from other centres of population. One might consider a city in the middle of Canada, Australia or China. Let us say that this art gallery has an extensive collection by a reasonably renowned local artist, and let us further assume that some of these works would fetch a reasonable amount if sold at auction. What is there to be said against the gallery selling one of these works (perhaps a relatively minor one) and spending the money on indiscernible copies of some canonical great paintings (together with an indiscernible copy of the painting that had been sold)? It is clear what could be said *for* this course of action: the residents of the city would appear to have the opportunity to have the experience they would have were they to look at the original versions of these paintings.

The first thought that might occur is that we do not have the technology to make perfect copies; the super Xerox machine is a philosophical myth. However, this is a merely technical limitation. We can frame our question as follows: were the technology to become available would it be right for the gallery to trade the relatively minor painting for a host of indiscernible copies? In other words, is the only thing to be said against this course of action a merely practical consideration? Indeed, one might even be sceptical about the objection; the technology of reproduction is now so advanced that, for at least some works, it *is* possible to create indiscernible copies. We could simply ship the various works into the gallery as the technology developed to copy them.

One might think, in framing a second objection, of the way in which I applied Wollheim's thought to forgeries above. After all, the products of our super Xerox machine do not feature marks that were placed there by the artist; when we look at the copy we are not looking at anything the artist produced. Indeed, it is highly probable that it was produced many years after the artist's death. We can break this thought into two objections: the first is that the original and not the copy was actually touched by the artist, and the second is that we would see the marks on the original as being placed there by the artist, and we would not see the marks on the copy in this way.

Does the fact that the original was worked on and touched by the artist make a difference? It certainly appears to give the work a certain aura; we seem to be able to reach out over the centuries and commune with Leonardo (or whomever). We need to be careful to distinguish two claims, however. What interests us is whether we are *justified* in taking the original as being more valuable as a painting than the copy. It might be that having been touched by the painter *causes* us to regard the painting in a special light, but that might not *justify* us in regarding it in a special light. Consider this parallel case. You might own a paperclip that was once owned by the Queen. This might lead you to keep it separate from other paperclips and perhaps even think of donating it to a museum. However, would you be *justified* in thinking that its value as a paperclip was greater than that of other paperclips? I would not have thought so. We can readily grant that it has some kind of talismanic value but that does not make it a better paperclip. Analogously, that the original was touched by Leonardo might cause us to regard it differently, not wanting to confuse it with any number of perfect copies. That is, we can grant that being touched by Leonardo gives the original *Mona Lisa* some kind of talismanic value; the question is whether that justifies our regarding it as a better painting. In parallel with the case of the paperclip, it is difficult to see that the mere historical connection is going to provide the justification.

The second objection looks more promising. When Leonardo started with the original *Mona Lisa*, all he had was an empty panel and some paint. He then marked the panel in such a way that we can now see the image on it. That is, he bought something new into the world: something of great artistic value. The copy did not bring anything new into the world; whatever is on the copy is there simply because it is on the original. It simply reproduces what was there before, so how can it be as valuable as the original? When we see the original, we see each of the marks as having been put there as a result of Leonardo's creativity. When we see the copy, all we see is the result of the technology of reproduction.

At first glance, this seems to provide us with the justification we need; it appears the original is more valuable than the copy. However, the distinction on which the argument turns cannot bear the weight that it is meant to bear. When we look at the original, we see what we see because that is what Leonardo painted. If he had painted something different, then we would see something different. This relation is known as "counterfactual dependence". Our experience of the painting is counterfactually dependent on Leonardo's actions; had his actions been different then our experience would have been different. This is the advantage the above argument claims the original has over the copy: in the original, "we see each of the marks as having been put there as a result of Leonardo's creativity". What undermines this argument is that exactly the same is true of the copy. Our experience of the copy is also counterfactually dependent on Leonardo's actions. The copy is exactly as it is because of Leonardo's actions; if his actions had been different, the copy would have been different in exactly this way (remember – we are considering a perfect copy).

Suppose that what we find valuable about the original is that it is beautiful and the painter's treatment of the subject matter is strikingly creative. This will be manifest in the painting. Everything about the painting that makes it beautiful and everything that makes it strikingly creative will survive in the copy; it will be as evident in the copy as it was in the original. The case is analogous to that of you creating a beautiful and strikingly original drawing on a computer and then printing a copy. Satisfied that it is what you want, you then photocopy it a dozen times. In this case, we do have the technology for making perfect copies. Nobody would claim that the copies that came out of the photocopier are any less valuable than that which came out of the printer. They are qualitatively identical to the original that came out of the printer; they are exactly as they are because that is what you drew. If you had drawn something different, the photocopies would have been different in exactly that way. Looking at the photocopies, what we see is your drawing.

What you have done with your drawing software is produce an image. It is the image that is the thing of value, and that image can be multiply produced: by the printer or by the photocopier (you could imagine printing directly from the photocopier if your computer was connected to it in the right way). Similarly, what we value in the *Mona Lisa* is the appearance that Leonardo produced (Sibley 2001). Technology being what it is, that appearance can only be manifested in one place: on the actual painting that he produced. However, as I said above, that is a merely technological limitation. If we had a super Xerox machine, we could make multiple copies of that image (it would have to be qualitatively identical to the *Mona Lisa* in every respect). In that case, it is difficult to see why, when we look at one of the copies, we are not seeing Leonardo's *Mona Lisa*.

In short, while there is clearly a talismanic difference between the original and the perfect copy, it is difficult to see why the latter should be thought less valuable as a painting. This suggests that the gallery mentioned earlier, the one remote from other centres of population, would be right to exchange an original for a set of perfect copies; it would give the population access to some canonical great paintings. Of course, there would still be a lot to sort out, not least being which paintings were the canonical great paintings or, indeed, whether the notion of there being "canonical great paintings" makes sense. However, it is difficult to see why the fact that what are being exhibited are *copies* in itself makes a difference. After all, nobody would think to object to the local library buying a copy of *War and Peace* on the grounds that what they are getting did not directly emerge from the hand of Tolstoy. What is of interest in the book – the novel – survives from copy to copy. What is of interest in the painting – the appearance – would also survive from copy to copy.

So far I have considered forgeries and perfect copies. I have argued that forgeries are not as valuable as the things they purport to be would have been, on the grounds that the forgery does not manifest the right sort of intentions (i.e. the intentions of the purported painter of the painting). A perfect copy, however, does manifest those intentions; it is counterfactually dependent on the intentions and actions of the artist. As I said at the beginning of this chapter, forgeries and copies are only two of a variety of related phenomena. The other phenomena throw up trickier and, I think, more interesting problems. In the remainder of this chapter we shall consider just one of those phenomena: a painting that appears simply to reproduce the image of a photograph.

The work in question is one of Gerhard Richter's cycle of paintings entitled *October 18, 1977*. The particular painting we shall look at is one of three that are entitled *Dead*. The story behind the painting is as follows. Between the late 1960s and 1998, a hard-left German terrorist group called The Red Army Faction (also known as the Baader-Meinhof Gang) committed various terrorist atrocities in Germany and beyond. By the mid-1970s, several of their members were in prison, including Ulrike Meinhof, Andreas Baader, Gudrun Ensslin, Jan-Carl Raspe and Irmgard Möller. After months of depression, Meinhof hanged herself on 9 May 1976, using a rope made from strips torn from a towel. As part of efforts to free their still-imprisoned colleagues, members of the gang still at large hijacked an aeroplane, subsequently killing its pilot. On 18 October, German police successfully ended the hijack as the plane waited on the runway in Mogadishu in Somalia. The news was relayed back to Germany. Later that day, Baader was found dead with a bullet wound to the back of his head, and Ensslin was found hanged in her cell. Raspe died later that day from another bullet wound to the head, and Möller was hospitalized with stab wounds to her chest, from which she later recovered. The circumstances surrounding these events remain controversial. This, in the context of a succession of murders and murder investigations, led to a great deal of questioning and national soul-searching.

The salient fact about Richter's cycle of paintings, at least for us, is the relation they bear to photographs. There are fifteen paintings in all, all based on photographs. The first (I shall describe them in turn, although the cycle was not intended to be exhibited in any particular order) is a rather sentimental portrait of a young Ulrike Meinhof. The next two are of the capture of another member of the gang, Holger Meins. Then there are three of a relaxed-looking Gudrun Ensslin. The seventh of the group is of Ensslin, hanged. Then there is a picture of Andreas Baader's cell and another of his record player (in which the revolver involved in his death was smuggled). The next two are of Baader, dead, and the following three (of which we will be looking at the second) are of Meinhof having been cut down from her improvised rope. Finally, there is the biggest picture of the group, based on a photograph of the funeral of Baader, Ensslin and Raspe.

Our example, entitled *Dead* (or sometimes *Dead 2* to distinguish it from its companion pieces) is relatively small: 62 cm × 62 cm. The three pictures are all based on the same photograph although there are subtle differences between them. Despite being the most distinct, *Dead 2* is slightly less grotesque; the throat is less accentuated, and the face seems less swollen. One might wonder why Richter painted several versions; perhaps something in the repetition hints at something that cannot be captured. The question on which I want to focus is why Richter based his painting on a photograph; what is the sense of painting an image that already exists in another medium? We can answer this question by answering another one: what is the difference between the painting and the photograph? Does the former mean something different from the latter and, if so, what and why?

In order to know to what we are comparing the painting, we need first to understand what it is to be a photograph. The image on which *Dead* was based was a police photograph, released to the press, a copy of which Richter had kept. Recent developments in technology – in particular, digital technology, which allows easy alteration of photographs – means we can no longer be sure that what we see in a photograph is what was in front of the lens when the photograph was taken. To clarify issues, let us focus on "ideal photographs", that is, photographs that have not been subject to undue manipulation (there is no reason to think that the photograph of Meinhof was manipulated).

Both the photograph and Richter's painting are of Meinhof. Of course, we might want to say that the painting is of a photograph of Meinhof (and that may or may not be right) but, in being so, it would also be of Meinhof. I am going to use the notion of a picture (painting or photograph) being *of* something in a relatively narrow sense. A picture is only *of* something if it gives us an image of that very thing. For example, it might be correct to say that a painting of a lamb *represents* Christ – it can do so allegorically – but it is not *of* Christ; rather, it is *of* a lamb.

With this in mind, we can isolate two prominent differences between a photograph and a painting. First, a painting can only be of something if (to put the matter roughly) the image looks like that thing. That is, to use a useful piece of philosophical jargon, the thing can be *seen in* the painting. If you look at a painting and all you can see in it is a fish, then it cannot be a painting of an elephant. A painting that is simply a blur cannot be a painting of anything apart from a blur. Photographs are different, however. If you manage to take a quick snap of a celebrity, then, even if the result is a grey blur that looks nothing like that celebrity, that photograph is still of that celebrity. You could be correct in pointing to the blur and saying (for example), "That is the Duke of Edinburgh". The following is roughly the account of what it is for a photograph to be of a particular thing (an X): a photograph is of an X if X caused the image on the photograph through the usual photographic means. Even more roughly, a photograph is of whatever was in front of the lens when the photograph was taken. The second prominent difference between photographs and paintings follows from this. That is (to use a term introduced earlier) photographs are counterfactually dependent on the visible world in front of the lens. The way the photograph looks depends on the way the world photographed looked. This is not true of paintings. Even if the mountain had looked different on that particular day, Cézanne may very well have still produced the painting that he did in fact produce. This is why photographs are evidence in a way that paintings are not. A court is likely to be a great deal more impressed by a photograph of the defendant holding up a bank than it would be with a pencil sketch of the defendant holding up a bank (Walton 2008).

Let us take a careful look at Richter's picture. At 62 cm × 62 cm it is bigger than the average photograph. It is also rather indistinct, even blurred (the lines of the original photograph are crisp). It shares some of the properties of the photograph. The image is clearly the same, and it is in black and white. Despite the blur, some of the details are not lost, in particular, the mark of the ligature around Meinhof's neck. The painting is, clearly, a copy of the photograph, although it differs in some ways from the photograph. This brings us back to our question: what is the difference between the painting and the photograph? Does the former mean something different from the latter and, if so, what and why?

Why would anyone want to produce a work of art, a painting, that is based on, or even looks like, a photograph? In Chapter 1, I discussed Danto's view that the difference between a work of art and a mere real thing was that the former was *about* something and the latter was not. Danto's example was Warhol's *Brillo Boxes*: Warhol's *Brillo Boxes* are about art; they assert that something can be a work of art and yet be perceptually indistinguishable from a mere real thing. The perceptually indistinguishable boxes in the store-room of the supermarket are not *about* anything at all; they just sit there containing Brillo pads. We can apply the same thought to this case. Let us grant, for the sake of argument, that the photograph and the painting capture the same image. This is the source of our puzzlement: why, if the photograph has perfectly captured the image, would we want to reproduce exactly the same image in paint? Danto's account offers us an answer to this. The photograph is about Meinhof in the sense that it is an image of Meinhof. Apart from that, however, it is not about anything; that is all that it is – an image. The painting is also about Meinhof in the sense that it is an image of Meinhof. It is also about many other things as well. It asserts, for example, that something can still be a painting even if it is a painting of a photograph.

However, this simply raises many more questions. Why would one want to produce an object that made the claim that something can be a painting even if it is a painting of a photograph? What would be the point? Once more, we need to go back to the modernist concept of the arts: the "second project" that started in the early twentieth century. In Chapter 1, I described the modernist view that the value of art, in particular painting, was thrown into doubt when it was criticized for "pedalling illusions". As we saw then, Greenberg attempted to rescue painting by urging practitioners "to entrench it more firmly in its area of competence" (1992: 308). For some people this provided a way of defending painting. For others it was too restrictive, too conservative, and thus painting became (and remains) the object of considerable suspicion by the avant-garde.

Danto argues that works of art get their content from the background "atmosphere of art theory", and that it is part of this theory that painting, as a medium, is problematic. Hence, if Danto is right, Richter's painting is, in part, about the problematic nature of painting. That is, Richter's photo-paintings are, in part, about how it is possible to produce paintings that escape at least some of the features of traditional paintings that are thought to be problematic. This, at least, is the view of one critic of Richter:

> Richter intends, on the one hand, to undermine representational painting but, on the other hand, to rescue it from the turbulent dis-course surrounding artistic practice during the second half of the twentieth century. Eschewing the traditional creative choices of composition, color, genre, and style, he transfers the fundamentals of photography, a relatively unburdened medium, to the painted representation. The black-and-white palette and "blurriness" are only the most obvious qualities of the paintings he began to pro-duce in the 1960s. Easily as important is the distance inherent in photography (*mediale Distanz*) that he borrows for his painting: the objectivity, mechanical production, and lack of creative composi-tion. For Richter, composition in photography follows a simple rule: "Composition is when the main person stands in the middle." And Richter's paintings present themselves as photographs, taking on as many characteristics of the medium as possible. In this way Richter has succeeded in producing works disengaged from the orthodox-ies of modern art, paintings that reject the formalism of Clement Greenberg and offer a new and different justification for a medium that had, in some quarters for more than a century, been repeatedly pronounced dead. Painting, then, was able to survive as photography in Richter's practice.   (Elger 2009: 52)

That is, one reason why Richter might want to produce a painting based on a photograph is that the painting is, in part, *about* how it is possible to res-cue painting by borrowing features from photography. Hence, the painting and the photograph are different works of art that are about different things: the photograph is simply about what it is a photograph of; the painting is about the justification of painting. Because the two works of art have differ-ent contents, it is possible that they have different values. The value of the experience of the one (had with understanding) is different from the value of the experience of the other (had with understanding).

This, of course, provides only a general way of showing how the value of a painting based on a photograph differs from that photograph; it does not tell us anything in particular about the work we are discussing – *Dead 2*. However, we might think there is a particular version of this general problem. If the medium of painting is problematic, then it can no longer perform one of its traditional functions: recording and memorializing significant historical events. A painting of the Baader-Meinhof Gang, if it were akin to (say) Franz Hals's *Banquet of the Officers of the St George Civic Company*, would look quite silly.

What, then, does being based on photographs bring to the paintings in the *October 18, 1977* cycle? Richter himself has said little about the paintings, but what he has said stresses two things and implies a third. The first and the second stand in some tension with each other or, at least, the first stresses the features of photography borrowed by the paintings and the second the features of the paintings besides those borrowed from photography. Both the first and the second draw on the distinction, described above, between a photograph and a painting.

The first of the points Richter makes draws on what we discussed above: using photographs to provide the "composition, color, genre, and style" of the painting. Asked whether he had considered "inventing images on this theme", as opposed to borrowing from photographs, Richter replied: "I think it is quite simply unthinkable to invent such pictures. That's just not possible nowadays. Painters used to train for years on end, to the point where they could to some extent invent nudes. That ability no longer exists. It's gone" (Richter 1995: 187).

This merely restates the general point. In particular, however, the fact that paintings borrow qualities from photographs enables them to carry the air of simply presenting, simply reporting, events. Clearly, the events depicted were among the most emotionally charged of recent German (indeed, European) history. Hence, it is difficult for the painter to achieve any distance: for the painting not to be seen as propaganda for one side or another. Photographs – particularly news photographs, on which the paintings were based – aspire to objectivity: to reporting without editorializing. The fact that Richter's paintings borrow some of these key features from photographs enables Richter to escape (to some extent) having to come down on one side of the political debate rather than the other. Richter draws attention in particular to their "lack of partisanship" (*ibid.*: 175): to the fact that, for him, painting is "reporting" (*ibid.*: 205).

If these are the qualities the paintings inherit from the photographs, there are also qualities they bring to the viewer's experience through being paintings. Intriguingly, Richter contrasts what a photograph is able to express with what a painting is able to express. Asked directly about the difference between the photograph and the painting, Richter says this: "Perhaps I can describe the difference like this: in this particular case, I'd say the photograph provokes horror, and the painting – with the same motif – something more like grief" (*ibid*.: 189). This is an assertion he repeats often in his writing: "[the paintings] are the almost forlorn attempt to give shape to feelings of compassion, grief and horror" (*ibid*.: 174); "[my viewpoint] is grief – compassion and grief" (*ibid*.: 200). Why is it that (to use Richter's contrast) a painting can be a vehicle for the expression of grief while a photograph can only express horror? This draws on the contrast above: a photograph is a recording of what was in front of the lens when the shutter was pressed while painting is the result of what the painter *does*. In looking at Richter's painting, we are not seeing the dead woman (a fit subject for horror); instead we are looking at an intentionally constructed image – a set of marks deliberately put on canvas. Richter could have done any number of things, but he chose to do this. We recognize his intention to memorialize a certain image in paint and, in recognizing this, come to see it as an expression of grief.

Above, I quoted the view that Richter's paintings present themselves as photographs, taking on as many characteristics of the medium as possible. This might suggest that when we are wondering about the value of Richter's paintings (whether or not they work as paintings) we should judge them in the same way as we judge a photograph. We have seen that the similarities between *Dead 2* and the photograph on which it was based enable the former to inherit some of the impartiality of the latter. However, we have also seen that the differences enable the former to convey something more than (or at least different from) the latter. This would already be enough to show that evaluating the painting is different from evaluating the photograph; we have to look, for example, at the painting's expressive qualities. Once again, this is clear from Richter's writings. When he writes about the works, he writes about them as paintings rather than as photographs. He thinks *Dead 2* "is calmer" than the others in the series; it cannot be the photographic image that is calmer because that is shared with two other paintings. He thinks one version of *Shot Man* "isn't that good", that is, not as good as the other version of *Shot Man*. Again, it cannot be the photographic image that is in question (Richter 1995: 198). Although in one sense the paintings are "copies of photographs", this does not make them the equivalent of those photographs. There is sense in having the paintings *as well* as the photographs. The photographs are valuable in providing an image; a horrific image of youthful idealism turned sour and leading to suicide. The paintings provide something else. The fact that they are based on photographs not only enables them to function in the turbulent world of avant-garde suspicion of paintings, but also the traditional values associated with painting reassert themselves. They are expressions of grief: monuments to a troubled time that need to be evaluated as paintings.

5. INTENTION AND INTERPRETATION

Louise Bourgeois's *Maman*

It is characteristic of avant-garde works of art over the past one hundred years that they are difficult to interpret. One problem with works of art being difficult to interpret – a problem that underlies some of the scepticism about the avant-garde – is that one does not know what such works conceal; content that is well worth excavating or a lacuna where content should be. However, it would be a mistake to associate difficulty exclusively with the recent and contemporary avant-garde; works of art have always been difficult to interpret. As we saw when we discussed aesthetic value in Chapter 2, to engage with a work one needs to understand it and understanding a work can be more difficult than it appears. On the one hand, a picture of a couple in a hotel bedroom might be just that and no more. On the other hand, it could take many hours or even years of patient study to understand what a painting is about. Paintings, at least great paintings, are not simply snapshots of appearances, to be understood and devoured in a matter of seconds.

The fact that interpreting a work of art can be subtle and difficult work raises a general question: what is it that distinguishes claims that are made about a work that are appropriate from those that are inappropriate? That is, what is it that distinguishes a sensible comment on a work of art from one that is not sensible? I shall consider this question with respect to one of the most enigmatic works of recent years: Louise Bourgeois' *Maman*. This work exists in several versions, not all of the same size. It has been displayed in various locations: in art galleries and in urban environments. The one I shall consider in particular was commissioned by Tate Modern in 1999. Tate Modern occupies a former power station and the first room visitors walk into is a truly vast turbine hall (it is 155 metres long and 35 metres [five stories] high). Bourgeois was the first artist commissioned to exhibit a work in the hall, the size of which clearly poses a problem. Although *Maman* was only part of what Bourgeois exhibited, it was the piece that captured the public's imagination. The spider is over nine metres high and is constructed from bronze and stainless steel with marble eggs contained in the sac that hangs beneath its body. What are we supposed to make of it? What are we supposed to make of the fact that the piece is called *Maman*?

Maman is a disconcerting object to confront. Spiders seem to have a special place in the human psyche, even for those who are not arachnophobic. The sculpture sits, apparently poised and malevolent, with uncertain intentions towards the spectator. Bourgeois, however, seemed to have no such effect in mind:

> The Spider is an ode to my mother. She was my best friend. Like a spider, my mother was a weaver. My family was in the business of tapestry restoration, and my mother was in charge of the workshop. Like spiders, my mother was very clever. Spiders are friendly presences that eat mosquitoes. We know that mosquitoes spread diseases and are therefore unwanted. So, spiders are helpful and protective, just like my mother. (Bourgeois, quoted in Tate 2008)

This view of spiders appears to be one she has held all her life. In an interview in 1968, she said, "I come from a family of repairers. The spider is a repairer. If you bash into the web of a spider she doesn't get mad. She weaves and she repairs it" (Coxton 2010: 68). Hence, we have two views or, at least, two places on a spectrum of views. On the one hand we have a perfectly understandable view from the spectator: that the sculpture is malevolent, even terrifying; and, on the other, the view of the artist – that it is helpful and protective, even nurturing. The question this raises is whether the artist's view trumps all the other views. That is, does Bourgeois' view give us the definitive interpretation of *Maman*? If she says that the sculpture is nurturing, then is anyone who takes the sculpture not to be nurturing simply wrong?

We need to be sure about which question we are answering. The issue here is what we need to understand in order to understand the work. We saw in Chapter 2 that it was necessary to understand a work in order to experience its value; if we experience a work without understanding, we are not valuing the work as a work. Also, as we saw in that chapter, sometimes we can engage with a work of art without understanding it. We might, for example, simply engage with the work because we like it or because it thrills us. Alternatively,

1. *Anthropometry* (ANT, 123) (1961) by Yves Klein (1928–62), Musée Cantini, Marseille, France/
Giraudon/The Bridgeman Art Library. © ADAGP, Paris and DACS, London 2012.

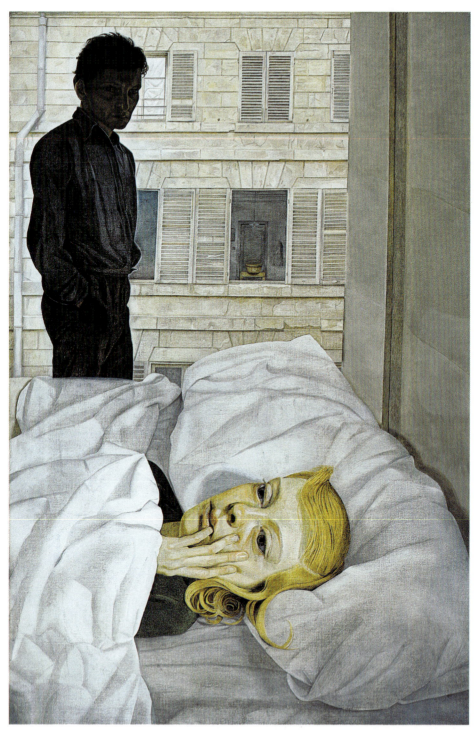

2. *Hotel Bedroom* (1954) by Lucian Freud (1922–2011). The Beaverbrook Foundation/The Beaverbrook Art Gallery, Fredericton, Canada. © The Lucian Freud Archive.

3. *Black on Maroon* (1958) by Mark Rothko (1903–70), acquisition: presented by the artist through the American Federation of Arts 1968, Reference T01031, Tate Modern, London. © Tate, London 2012 and © 1998 Kate Rothko Prizel and Christopher Rothko ARS, NY and DACS, London.

4. *Dead 2* (1988) by Gerhard Richter (b. 1932), Museum of Modern Art, New York. Digital Image © 2012, The Museum of Modern Art, New York/Scala, Florence. © Atelier Gerhard Richter 2012.

5. *Maman* (1999) by Louise Bourgeois (1911–2010), as installed in Tate Modern Turbine Hall, London. © Tate, London 2012/Louise Bourgeois Trust/DACS, London/VAGA, New York 2012.

6. *Three Studies for Figures at the Base of a Crucifixion* (1944) by Francis Bacon (1909–92), Tate Gallery, London. © Tate, London 2012.

7. *Nighthawks* (1942) by Edward Hopper (1882–1967), Art Institute of Chicago. Photography © The Art Institute of Chicago.

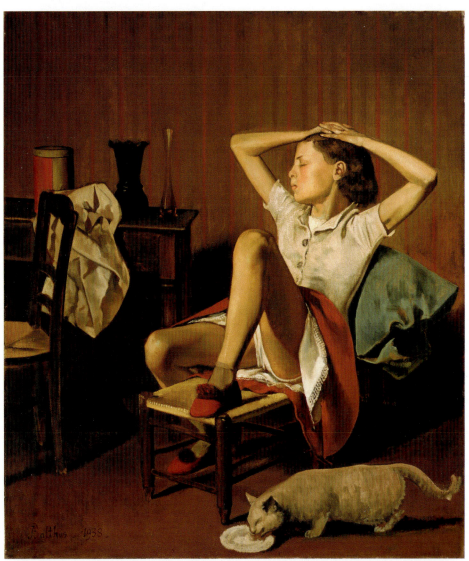

8. *Thérèse Dreaming* (1938) by Balthus (Klossowski de Rola, Balthasar) (1908–2001). Metropolitan Museum of Art, New York. © 2012. Image copyright The Metropolitan Museum of Art/Art Resource/Scala, Florence.

we might simply be interested in the way the work *strikes* us. Some person, on seeing *Maman*, might find it malevolent and terrifying. They can truly say – of course – that the sculpture *strikes them* as malevolent and terrifying. This, however, is not what we are interested in (at least, not directly). Recall the two reactions to the cricket game we looked at in Chapter 2: those of the knowledgeable Josh and those of the rather clueless Jim. As we saw, Jim can rightly claim to like cricket and can talk with authority about how a particular game struck him. However, if someone wanted to know facts about the game – how the game went and whether it was, compared to other games that season, a good game – Jim's report would be of no use to them. Facts about how the game struck Jim are of purely biographical interest (if of any interest at all); people generally want to know about the game itself. If they want to know about the game itself, they need to ask someone who understands the game: that is, they need to ask Josh rather than Jim.

Our question, then, is not about how *Maman* strikes us. Rather, what we want to know is what we need to understand if we are to appreciate it with understanding. This takes us into controversial territory and into some characteristic disputes between the philosophy of art and cognate disciplines such as art history and art theory. Although philosophers are generally happy to talk about "the message" of a work or what a work of art "means", such an approach is seldom taken by the other disciplines. The alternative is to allow that a work might have multiple interpretations or that the work's meaning may not be stable; as soon as one has settled on some meaning, some other aspect of the work may emerge to undermine it. However, the philosophical approach is a great deal more flexible than it appears. As we saw in Chapter 2, the correct understanding of a work might be that it is ambiguous or that it is indeterminate. Furthermore, it is possible that a work may not have a single correct understanding or, if it does, a single correct understanding need not fix a single correct evaluation (Budd 1995: ch. 1). In addition, the fact that one task of criticism is to seek to understand a work and make judgements does not mean that this is the *only* task of criticism. We can afford to be pluralists and admit that works of art support a range of different critical projects. Some such projects might resist the attempt to "close down" our interaction with the work by talking of its message and instead allow a wide range of responses loosely tied to the work's content.

The project that interests us here, however, is that of attempting to understand the work so as to open the door to making judgements about the work. To adopt some useful terminology from Levinson, we are attempting to find the work's "primary meaning" (Levinson 1996a: 272–3). As well as giving us an account of what it is to understand the work (what it is to understand the work is to grasp its primary meaning), postulating such a meaning makes sense of other aspects of critical practice. It makes sense of the thought that there are more-or-less appropriate things we can say about a work. Saying that *Maman* is expressive is clearly more appropriate than saying that *Maman* is not expressive. The former is part of the primary meaning in a way that the latter is not. Having a notion of the primary meaning of a work also makes sense of the thought that our grasp of a work can improve, rather than just change. Our grasp improves the closer we get to the primary meaning. This is not, however, to pretend that the notion is pellucid; exactly what is meant by "the primary meaning" will only emerge in the discussion below.

Specifying the primary meaning of a work can be a complicated task that involves asking several different questions. First, it needs to be established whether what we have before us has a primary meaning at all; that is, whether it is a proper object for interpretation. Versions of *Maman* have been installed in unexpected settings such as on a pavement and in woodland. Were we to come across *Maman* in one of these settings it might be unclear exactly what its function is. Is it merely a bird-scarer? A misplaced piece of salvage? If it were either of those two things there would be no primary meaning to investigate (I am assuming that bird-scarers and salvage are not *about* anything). Hence, we need to settle the question as to whether what we have in front of us is a proper object of interpretation (which, in practice, means asking whether what we have in front of us is *a work in some art form or other*).

Let us assume that we have established that what we have in front of us is art and therefore the proper object of interpretation. We would then need to establish where exactly the boundaries of the object to be interpreted lie. When *Maman* was first exhibited at Tate Modern it was alongside three welded steel towers. Should we be looking for the primary interpretation of the spider considered on its own, or some composite work of the spider and the three towers? That is, does the work include the spider and the three towers, or are they two (or three or four) works that just happened to be exhibited together? Different answers to this question might well result in different accounts of primary meaning.

Once we have settled the questions of whether a work is a proper object of interpretation and what are its boundaries, the third question we can ask concerns the correct category in which to consider the work. The idea that artworks are evaluated within categories is due to Walton (1987). Walton thought that we are at a loss to know what to look for in evaluating a work until we know what kind of work it is that we are evaluating. If *Maman* is within the category of sculpture, the properties to which we need to attend in evaluating it are dictated by the properties characteristic of sculpture (e.g. sculptures tend to be free-standing and thus independent of context). If it is within the category of installation, our evaluation will be dictated by the properties characteristic of installation works (e.g. such works are not independent of context). As there are many different versions of the work in the world, a single instance of the work could even be judged against the work's other instances: that is, judged within the category of *Mamans*. The *Maman* exhibited in San Francisco, for example, was *small for a Maman*. The same work could be judged unintimidating in the category of *Mamans* yet intimidating in the category of sculptures.

We have, then, three questions. Is it a proper object of interpretation? What are its boundaries? In what category should it be judged? Once these three have been settled, we are left with the fourth question: what does the work mean? The correct answer to these questions with respect to particular works of art is a matter for an art critic or art historian. Such disciplines can tell us whether *Maman* is a work of art, what in fact is or is not included in the work, whether it is appropriate to judge it as a sculpture or an installation piece and, finally, what the work means. The philosophical issues are *the grounds to which we should appeal* in coming up with those answers. That is, we are not so much interested in settling the issues with respect to this particular work of art as finding out what we need to appeal to in order to settle the issues.

Let us consider each of our questions in turn. What would make it the case that an object we encounter is a proper object of interpretation? That is, what makes it the case that "What does this mean?" is the right question to ask about the object? What makes it the case that we are being asked to consider it as a piece of sculpture rather than as a bird-scarer? In Chapter 1, we saw that, according to what I there called "the modernist definition of art", something is a work of art if someone intends it to be interpreted within the web of relations of art theory and art history. If this is right, then the question as to whether what we had before us was a proper object of appreciation would be settled by ascertaining whether anyone had actually intended that it be taken as one. This is not the only view. Other philosophers, notably Walton, have argued that if a society generally treats something as a proper object of interpretation, then it is a proper object of interpretation, whether or not anyone ever had the appropriate intention (Walton 1990: ch. 1). One way to sort out where your intuitions stand on this matter is to consider a particular scenario. Imagine going into an artist's studio after his or her death, and finding a paint-smeared canvas on the floor. What would make it the case that this was a work of art? Would it be that the artist intended it to be taken as a work of art? Or would it be enough that society came to regard it as a work of art? If your intuitions go with the former, you have intentionalist leanings; if the latter, you do not.

Intentions are also an obvious thing to which to appeal in answering questions concerning the boundaries of a work of art. The works of Shakespeare come to us through two sources: the original Quarto editions and the 1623 collection called the "First Folio". The texts in the Quarto sometimes differ substantially from the First Folio versions. What, then, would make it the case that a certain speech was or was not part of *King Lear*? Once again, a plausible answer would be to defer to the author. If we could speak to Shakespeare, his word would settle the issue. If he said the speech was in it would be part of the work, and if he said it was out it would not be part of the work. Alternatively, one could argue that what settles the boundaries is what would make the work artistically more successful. If the speech improves *Lear*, it is part of *Lear*; otherwise it is not. One problem with this view is that there might be many scenes, canonically thought to be part of a play, that seem not to improve it (the porter scene in *Macbeth* being one example). On such a view, these scenes would not be part of the plays at all.

If the answers to the previous two questions are not decisively settled, the answer to the third – the correct category in which to judge the work – is even less clear-cut. On this issue, Levinson is an intentionalist; the correct category in which to interpret a work is determined by the actual intentions of the actual author (Levinson 1996b: 188–9). Hence, for Levinson, there would be some fact of the matter as to whether or not *Maman* was or was not an installation piece, the fact being determined by the content of Bourgeois' intention. Walton himself is more circumspect, listing the author's intentions as one of a number of determining factors (albeit a matter of "crucial importance") (Walton 1987: 72). The flexibility Walton advocates is welcome, as there seem to be clear cases of works of art for which the category does not depend on intentions. If I write a poem of fourteen lines of iambic pentameter, divided into three quatrains and a couplet, then I have written a sonnet, whatever I might have thought I was doing.

Irrespective of whether the appropriate category is always determined by the artist's intentions or could be determined by other factors, Levinson and Walton agree that we (the audience) cannot simply put the work in whatever category would suit it best. Of course, if we are watching a dire film we might make is *seem* better by viewing it in the category "satire" (this might, for example, be the sensible way to approach Paul Verhoeven's *Showgirls*). However, to make a work *seem* better than it is is not to make it *be* better than it is. We cannot allow the audience the power to make works better than they are.

It is plausible, then, that the correct answer to the first three of our four questions is determined (or largely determined) by the actual intentions of the author. This leaves us with the remaining question. Having settled that what we have before us is a proper object of interpretation, what is part of the work and what not and, finally, the appropriate category under which to judge the work, we need to settle the primary meaning of the work. There is a simple and obvious thought as to why we should stay with the actual intentions of the artist as that which determines what the work means. Works of art are, very broadly, forms of communication. Bourgeois, in her studio, felt the urge to say something: to communicate something to the world. She carried out her plan by making *Maman*. Works of art are just like any other communicative acts; understanding a work of art, like understanding a sentence that a person utters, is a matter of grasping what it is the person is trying to communicate.

Sometimes this view – which, as it deals with the actual intentions of the artist, is called "actual intentionalism" – seems obviously correct. For example, a line in Roy Campbell's poem "Buffel's Kop" is sometimes printed as "… all heaven in the pale/Roaring …" and sometimes as "… all heaven in the gale/Roaring …". What makes it the case that "gale" rather than "pale" is correct is that "gale" is the word Campbell intended ("pale" slipped in as a typographical error). There are some questions that a critic could ask that are best answered by appeal to actual intentions. However, there are good reasons to doubt that it is the complete, or even the central, account of what governs interpretation. First, we can question the premise I slipped in above: that works of art are "forms of communication". That is, I claimed above that works of art are vehicles for some message the artist wants to communicate, and that the meaning of a work of art just is that message. The problems with this can be summed up in a nice example by Monroe Beardsley:

> A man says, "I like my secretary better than my wife"; we raise our eyebrows, and inquire: "Do you mean that you like her better than you like your wife?" And he replies, "No, you misunderstand me; I mean I like her better than my wife does." Now in one sense he has cleared up the misunderstanding, he has told us what he meant. Since what he meant is still not what the first sentence succeeded in

> meaning, he hasn't made the original sentence any less ambiguous than it was; he has merely substituted for it a better, because unambiguous one.   (Beardsley 1981: 25)

Beardsley's example draws a neat distinction between the meaning of the sentence and the author's intention. The first sentence has two meanings, irrespective of the fact that the speaker intended only one of them. Even when what the speaker meant has been resolved, the sentence retains its ambiguity; what *it* means is not fixed by the intentions of the speaker. Similarly, we can allow that, in making *Maman*, Bourgeois was attempting to communicate her feelings about her mother. As with the ambiguous sentence, we need to ask whether *Maman* actually means what Bourgeois intended it to mean and, like the sentence, if it does not, then what the work means and what Bourgeois means will come apart.

The core of the anti-intentionalist argument rests on a deeply held intuition about our engagement with art: it is not possible for the meaning of a work of art to go beyond the conclusions of our best critical practices. The argument is of the same form as one used against certain forms of strong moral realism. Consider the view that the truths of morality are fixed independently of our best moral practices. If this were the case then it would be possible that, unbeknown to us, gratuitously causing pain is in fact right rather than wrong. The argument against strong moral realism is that this thought makes no sense; there is no "moral reality" out there, independent of our moral beliefs and practices. Analogously, the meaning of a work of art cannot be something that lies beyond our best critical beliefs and practices. If the meaning of a work is given by the intentions of the artist, and if the intentions of the artist are something that might be forever inaccessible to us, then the meaning of the work might forever be inaccessible to us. The thought is that this is simply implausible; the meanings of works do not lie in some hidden realm. They are part of the work and what we are getting at when we engage with the work.

What alternative is there to actual intentionalism? One view was famously articulated by Beardsley himself, writing with his colleague, W. K. Wimsatt (Wimsatt & Beardsley 1976). This paper, one of the most reproduced in philosophy, is a hotchpotch of different views and arguments, and it is not always clear what precisely is being claimed. I shall pick on two lines of thought within the paper. For the first, we shall have to change our example from the visual arts to poetry (or indeed to any art form that relies on the written word). There is a form of meaning that we can call "word sequence meaning". This is the meaning (or meanings) of a sentence worked out using the dictionary meanings of the words and the language's grammar. We can index this meaning to the time at which the sentence was written, but, apart from that, it is independent of context. Can we identify the meaning of a work of poetry or literature with its word sequence meaning?

Consider an example: Dylan Thomas's line "The force that through green fuse drives the flower/Drives my green age". It is clear that attempting to elicit what we are supposed to understand by this armed only with a dictionary and a grammar would be quixotic. The reason is not hard to find. We are rarely interested in word sequence meaning on its own, but rather as a means to something richer: what someone meant by something on some particular occasion. What did Dylan Thomas mean by putting those words in that order? What was he trying to get across? We need to supplement word sequence meaning with something else in order to grasp what is meant; hence, inasmuch as Wimsatt and Beardsley were attempting to equate the meaning of some literary work with word sequence meaning, their argument fails. The problem is thrown into even greater relief if we attempt to apply the view to examples in the visual arts. Language exhibits compositionality: that is, we build up the meaning of larger units (sentences) out of smaller units (words). The visual arts do not exhibit compositionality; or at least they do not do so simply and systematically. Patches of colour (or, more accurately, volumes in pictorial space) are not themselves semantic units for which there are grammars to guide how we might construct them into larger semantic units. Similarly, parts of *Maman* do not combine, through some analogy of grammatical rules, into the meaning of the work.

We could attempt a weaker claim that captures the spirit of Wimsatt and Beardsley's position. We can attempt to draw a boundary between what is part of the work and what is not. Wimsatt and Beardsley's position is that, in determining the interpretation of the work, critics must draw only on features that are part of the work and not on features that lie outside it. This entails a respect for that deeply held intuition discussed earlier. Everything that is part of the work will be available to our best critical practices; we simply have to scrutinize the work and we will find it there (this underlies Wollheim's naming the position "the scrutiny view"). Things that lie outside the work (including intentions) may not be available. Hence, if criticism draws only on features that are part of the work, it will always have everything that it needs for interpretation.

There are a number of problems with this. First, it is very difficult to draw a boundary between what is part of the work and what is not. Many terms in English refer to things in the world: "the Cadogan Hotel", "the Indian Mutiny", "the Armenian Question". The meaning of referring terms at least involves their referents, and their referents are clearly not within the work but outside in the world. Wimsatt and Beardsley's own attempt to draw a boundary is spectacularly unsuccessful for these and other reasons (Wimsatt & Beardsley 1976: 6–7).

Second, the view is underspecified. We are told we need to "draw on features that are part of the work". There are, however, many features that are part of the work that will not be relevant. It is of no help being told we need to scrutinize the work unless we are told what we are scrutinizing the work *for*. Until we are told that, we are as much in the dark as to what to do as someone is who is told to make something "average sized". Consider, for example, the features of a work that belong to its causal, rather than the intentional, history. These are the kinds of features that it is appropriate to look for in natural objects; we can scrutinize cliff faces for features that reveal whether the cliff is a product of erosion or of movement in a geological fault. We can also scrutinize works of art for such features: there are historians of ink, of paper and of pigments who are interested in the causal history of what they have before their eyes. However, that is not what Wimsatt and Beardsley have in mind. In interpreting a work, of course, we are scrutinizing it for *meaning*, and meaning belongs to the intentional rather than the causal history of the object. Only things that have been created have meanings, and finding meanings is finding the patterns of intention of the creator. This leaves Wimsatt and Beardsley's view in a rather unstable position. Even if we can make sense of only taking into consideration features that are part of the work, it is nonetheless the case that what we are looking for in the features that are part of the work are traces of intention. We shall see shortly that this might not be the actual intentions of the actual creator of the work – and that might be enough to placate Wimsatt and Beardsley – but we are in the realms of the intentional nonetheless.

The third problem with Wimsatt and Beardsley's view is that it encounters the same problems we encountered in Chapter 2 when we attempted to draw a distinction between what is part of the content of perception and what we infer from perception. The claim I am attributing to Wimsatt and Beardsley is that critics must draw only on features that are part of the work and not on features that lie outside it. However, knowing something about the work (some piece of outside information) may well bring us to experience the work differently. *Paradise Lost* (to take a famous example) is a poem that deals with the civil war among the angels and the fall of Satan. At the time at which he wrote it, Milton was Cromwell's Latin secretary. Knowing this piece of information brings one to experience in Milton's verse echoes of the English Civil War and its tragic consequences. Our beliefs about the circumstances in which a work was produced (which Wimsatt and Beardsley would regard as external and hence critically irrelevant) affect our experience of the work (which Wimsatt and Beardsley would regard as internal and hence critically relevant). That is, something that seems to be external – merely an additional belief – can make a difference to the content of what we experience and thus become internal. Our experiences can be altered by our beliefs so the boundary Wimsatt and Beardsley are attempting to draw cannot be drawn.

To be fair to Wimsatt and Beardsley, they are aware that background knowledge can change the way we experience a work. In one of their examples, they consider a metaphor from a poem by John Donne. The knowledge that Donne was interested in "the new astronomy" leads one critic (Charles Coffin) to interpret the metaphor as alluding to that science. However, Wimsatt and Beardsley are resolute that to do this is to "disregard the English language" (Wimsatt & Beardsley 1976: 9). If one has – as they do – a conception of the work as *given* in experience, then anything we bring to it that will *alter* that experience will pollute the "true" (unaltered) experience of the work. This certainly is a danger; external information (whether biographical facts about the creator, or facts about who owns a work, or facts about how much it is worth) can make a clear-sighted experience of the work difficult. It is difficult, although surely desirable, not to let our knowledge of the tragic nature of Rothko's life infect our experience of his paintings. That, however, is a distinct issue. That external information *can* distort our experience does not mean that *all* such changes are a distortion. To insist that a clear-sighted experience of *Paradise Lost* requires us to isolate or ignore our knowledge of Milton's life not only asks the impossible, but is also unmotivated; why not engage with a work using all the resources at our disposal?

We have seen that both actual intentionalism and anti-intentionalism are untenable. What, then, is the answer? Are there any firm philosophical foundations for criticism? One further option emerges out of elements of both the views that we have rejected. The problem with actual intentionalism was that it opened a potential gap between our best critical practices and the meaning of a work. The problem with Wimsatt and Beardsley's view is the lack of any positive account of what it is to find meaning in a work. We need to preserve Wimsatt and Beardsley's insight that the meaning is located in the work and not the head of the creator, and actual intentionalism's insight that meaning is a matter of tracing patterns of intention. That is, we look for patterns of intention *in the work* and do not ask the further question as to whether these were the actual intentions of the actual author.

This view, known as "hypothetical intentionalism" is associated with William Tolhurst (1979) and Levinson (1996b). According to hypothetical intentionalism, the primary meaning of a work (here a literary work) is given by "the best hypothesis, from the position of an appropriately informed, sympathetic, and discriminating reader, of authorial intent to convey such and such to an audience, through the text in question" (Levinson 2006b: 302). Put rather more roughly, what we do in attempting to understand a work is take a "best guess" as to what the author intended to convey to their audience. This does not open the gap that threatened actual intentionalism because the meaning of the work is given by the "best guess", and the "best guess" is the outcome of our best critical practices. Unlike Wimsatt and Beardsley, it also provides a positive account of what it is to find meaning in a work: we make a guess, from what we have before us, as to what the author was intending to convey. Actually, although I have portrayed Wimsatt and Beardsley as providing no positive view, a version of this theory can be found in their paper. However, as their version is both sketchy and flawed, I have focused on their more sceptical (and more familiar) arguments.

In a moment, I shall look at some examples of hypothetical intentionalism at work, including *Maman*. Before that, however, one more aspect of the theory needs to be sorted out. Above, I argued that some items of "external information" can affect our experience of a work. I also pointed out that Wimsatt and Beardsley regard this as dangerous: as bringing with it the possibility of reading things into the work that are not really there. I agreed this was a possibility, but disagreed that it should drive us to a blanket ban on all external information. Instead, we should simply guard against such misreading. What is hypothetical intentionalism's position in this debate?

The theory itself does not take a stand one way or the other. All it requires is that we take a "best guess" as to what the author intended to convey to their audience. The work itself is the basis for such a best guess; what other information we can use is not settled. Clearly, how much external information we can use lies on a continuum. We could specify that only the bare minimum of information should be used: only information "internal" to the work (however we are able to specify that). At the other extreme, we could specify that we can use any and all the information we have about the author, the work and the circumstances of its production. Adopting some useful terminology from Levinson, let us call the first of these the "thinly" specified author and the latter, the "thickly" specified author (Levinson 1996c: 229). Let us take "Fern Hill" by Dylan Thomas as our example. If the aim of the hypothetical intentionalist was only to construct the intentions of a thinly specified author they would ask (roughly), "What is my best guess about what the author of this was trying to convey – whoever they happened to be?" If they were trying to construct the intentions of a thickly specified author, they would ask (roughly), "what is my best guess about what Dylan Thomas meant by this, given that (a) he grew up on a farm called "Fern Hill", (b) the writing of the poem was possibly spurred by his house being machine-gunned by a jealous husband, (c) he worked on the poem for many years and that it existed in many versions?" (and so on).

As will be clear by my argument above concerning the legitimacy of employing our knowledge of Milton's employment during the English Civil War, I would favour the thickly specified author. The only reason for not doing so is Wimsatt and Beardsley's worry about reading things into the poem that are not really there. However, as I have argued, we can guard against that. We seem to have something like an answer to the question: what makes something an appropriate interpretation of a work? The answer is, roughly, that something is an appropriate interpretation of a work if it is part of the best guess as to what the thickly specified author might have intended to be grasped by the audience at which the work was aimed. Provided that what we are after is what earlier we called "the primary meaning" of the work, this seems to me along the right lines. However, there is one potential problem we need to consider before we are in the clear.

The problem lies in whether an author can be *too* thickly specified. Consider a scenario in which part of the external information of which we are aware is statements by the author about what he or she intended the work to mean. Let us say, to paint things in black and white, that our best critical practices without this information would have resulted in our saying the work meant one thing, and the author's stated view is that the work means something different. If we allow the author's view to count despite what we would have got out of the work, we seem to be back to actual intentionalism: there is a gap opening up between what the work would mean without knowledge of intentions and what it means with knowledge of those intentions (Stecker 1997: 200–202).

There are a number of things the hypothetical intentionalist could do here. One option would be to stop before the author gets too thickly specified: to not allow the author's stated intentions about the work to count. They could escape the charge that this is flagrantly *ad hoc* by appeal to what critics actually do; to consult the author's intentions in this way would be against "the ground rules of the game of literary decipherment" (Levinson 1996b: 208). However, Robert Stecker offers another, and I think better, option. This is to allow that the author's views about their intentions count, but simply to throw them into the mix alongside everything else. After all, all they have given us is their view about what they were doing. If the situation is one in which the work looks as if it is not the product of that intention, but of a different intention, this would suggest that their view about what they were doing is incorrect. That is, we allow that their statements about their own intentions are one guide to their intentions, but that what is actually in the work is also a guide: furthermore, a guide that may well be more reliable than that provided by external knowledge.

This might appear far-fetched. Surely we are the best authority about our own intentions? Surely (for example) Bourgeois knew what she was doing, and hence her statement as to her intentions should not just be taken as one more piece of evidence to ground our "best guess" as to what she was up to? We are the best authority about our own intentions in many circumstances but there are some perfectly ordinary circumstances in which we are not. Someone may genuinely believe that they are acting in someone else's best interests when it is apparent to everyone else that their real intentions are governed by self-interest. We do not need to appeal to marginal real-life cases, however; the creation of art is itself a special case where artists are unlikely to have a very clear idea as to what they are doing. A simple communication view of art, where the artist has some clear idea in his or her head prior to the creation of art and the task is simply to create something to be the vehicle for that idea, is simply not plausible as a general account of artistic endeavour. Of course, it will sometimes be true. A more typical case, however, will be where the artist has a rather inchoate view of what he or she wants to do, and then works with the medium to make that view more concrete. The creative process, mysterious as it is, draws on all the parts of the mind, conscious and unconscious. In such cases, there is reason to trust what is produced as a more reliable guide to intention than the artist's conscious assessment as to what they have done.

Let us try to pull the threads of the discussion together by drawing again on our example. Faced with Bourgeois' sculpture as one walks into the Turbine Hall, I claimed, one is likely to find the piece malevolent and terrifying. However, there are many facts that one can take into account in hypothesizing the intentions of the "thickly specified" author. First, throughout her creative life, Bourgeois has been intensely interested in psychoanalysis and the symbols of the creative unconscious. Second, Bourgeois has produced spiders in various forms, some of them rather benign. Third, when one looks at what she has said about her work, one not only learns of the link with her mother but also that her adopted son (who died young) apparently valued spiders as a protection against mosquitoes. I am not sure that this information transforms the experience, but certainly looking at *Maman* as something protective is a different experience from looking at it as something threatening. Indeed, understanding the work of art, like understanding any worthwhile work of art, is going to be a complex matter: my own view is that one's experience oscillates between seeing the work as benign and the threat and malevolence that are always edging to break through. This, of course, reflects psychoanalysis's reconstruction of our attitude to our parents in our early years.

Encountering *Maman* is a rich perceptual experience that those who visited the Turbine Hall are unlikely to forget. I am going to end this chapter by looking at a strong thread that has run through what in Chapter 1 I called "the modernist definition of art". To remind ourselves, this began around the beginning of the twentieth century with works such as Duchamp's *Fountain*: a barely altered, ordinary urinal. As I said in Chapter 1, it is not the object itself that should be the focus of our attention. Considered as an object, it is no more interesting than any other urinal (except in the sense that the Queen's paperclip becomes, through this fact alone, more interesting than any other paperclip). What is interesting is Duchamp's gesture, or the thought behind the gesture, of which the object itself is only a trace.

Let us put this thought together with a thought that has been around at least since the time of Immanuel Kant. Kant thought that genius was necessary for the production of great art: "genius … is a talent for producing that for which no definite rule can be given: and not an aptitude in the way of cleverness for what can be learned according to some rule" (Kant 1952: §46). Together these thoughts from Duchamp and Kant do not entail, but they do suggest, a division of artistic labour. First, there is the idea: the inspiration. Second, there is the work involved in making the work: in making the idea manifest. The first corresponds to genius and is the true test of the artist. The second is merely mechanical skill (or "aptitude"). Putting the matter bluntly, the artist is the genius who has the idea; actually making something in the world that corresponds to that idea is merely a matter of engineering. These were the kinds of thought (whether or not from these specific sources) that underpinned one of the more extreme manifestations of the modernist avant-garde: Conceptual Art.

"Conceptual Art" named an artistic movement that flourished from around 1966 to 1977. Without the capital letters, it names an approach to art exemplified in some of Duchamp's work and running through much of the twentieth and twenty-first centuries. Its underlying idea, which matches the two stages of making art just identified, was stated clearly and succinctly by Sol LeWitt: "In conceptual art the idea or concept is the most important aspect of the work. When an artist uses a conceptual form of art, it means that all of the planning and decisions are made beforehand and the execution is a perfunctory affair" (LeWitt 1993: 834). An extreme, but not altogether uncharacteristic, example would be the Dutch artist Stanley Brouwn's work, which consisted of all the shoe shops in Amsterdam (Godfrey 1998: 119). Such art appears to raise the problem of the role of the intentions of the artist in a particularly pure form. If the idea is the most important aspect of the work, and the outward manifestation (if there is an outward manifestation) is "perfunctory", how do we grasp the work in all its glorious complexity? There seems little sense in directing our best critical practices towards something perfunctory instead of towards what is really important, namely, the idea. That is, our efforts would best be directed at grasping the idea directly. The obvious way to do so would be simply to ask the artist. However, as we have already seen in this chapter, such a simple actual intentionalism is unsatisfactory.

Some of the ideas discussed in Chapter 1 go some way to providing a solution to this apparent problem. There I quoted Danto's view that the content of art was provided by "something the eye cannot descry – an atmosphere of artistic theory, a knowledge of the history of art: an artworld" (Danto 1995: 209). We saw that such relations gave Warhol's *Brillo Boxes* a content that supermarket Brillo boxes lacked. Such relations can also give content to a work of conceptual art (whether we take that to be the idea or its perfunctory manifestation). Thus, to take the example of Brouwn's work, we need focus neither on simply grasping the idea nor on how the idea is manifested. Instead, we focus on the relation between the idea and the art theory of the time: what is Brouwn saying about art? To what is it a reaction? Where does it fit into the ongoing "conversation"?

The optimistic view, then, is that we can escape having to appeal directly to intentions by focusing on the work and its relation to its art world context; this is something accessible, if not to the eye, then at least to the mind (Duchamp repeatedly said that he wanted to "put art in the service of the mind"). Although I argued in Chapter 1 that relational accounts of art such as that of Danto do seem to capture at least some aspects of the modernist concept of art, it is not clear that such accounts can altogether get us out of having to appeal to intentions. The problem is that the account is ungrounded. We grasp the content of the work of art by looking at where it sits in the network of relations of art theory and art history, but what fixes the nature of those relations? Let us stick with our example of Conceptual Art. The history of art (or, at least, of avant-garde art) in the 1950s and 1960s can be told in a variety of ways. On the surface, there seemed a bewildering variety of "isms" passing in fairly short order: abstract expressionism, minimalism, and Conceptual Art (with pop art fitting in somewhere). The correct way to interpret these developments is controversial. Conceptual Art has been seen as a logical development of minimalism (objects getting ever more minimal). An alternative view is that it is a *rejection* of minimalism and a reassertion of the value of high art. However, unless we can agree on some way to interpret these developments, we are not going to get anything determinate when we look at the relation between the individual works and the network of relations: the question will always be, how do we interpret the network of relations? The obvious way to fix on the correct interpretation of the network of relations is to work it out from the meanings of the works. However, we now have two unknowns with only one equation: we are using the works to fix the correct interpretation of the network of relations, and the network of relations to fix the correct interpretation of the works. It looks as if we are going to have to appeal to something else, which takes us back to intention.

The appeal to intentions raises the question asked near the beginning of this chapter: in asking for a determinate primary meaning, are philosophers asking the right question? Instead of seeking to fix meanings, what we have to undergo is a balancing act: we think of ways to interpret the network of relations that make best sense of the work, and ways of interpreting the work that make best sense of the network of relations. This easygoing compromise looks attractive, but it does not come without cost. Instead of *discovering* the meaning of a work of art, we *construct* it. What a work means does not depend on its creator, but rather on our interpretative efforts. Different views on the meaning of a work are not correct or incorrect, but simply more or less appropriate. The artist, and the intentions of the artist, can be trumped by the stories we weave as critics: stories that are themselves always up to being replaced by better stories. The "institutional" solution to the "problem of conceptual art" results, then, in a loss of the distinctive primary meaning for these works of art. This might be more of a cost than we are prepared to bear.

101

However, there is another possibility, which is to deny that conceptual art does represent a radical break with the past. That is, the critic is still right to apply the methods they would apply to any other work of art (this is the view taken by several of the contributors to Goldie & Schellekens [2007]). My own view is not optimistic; there are too many works of conceptual art that do not provide enough for the critic to scrutinize so as to hypothesize as to what the artist intended. The difficulty is brought out by Wollheim in his essay "Minimal Art" (1973a). Wollheim considers two works: Duchamp's *Fountain* and one of Ad Reinhardt's *Black Canvasses* (that is, a series of canvasses that have largely undifferentiated black surfaces). I shall consider only his discussion of the Reinhardt work. Wollheim characterizes the traditional conception of a work of art (which dovetails with the traditional conception of our engaging with an appreciating art) as follows: "A man starts with a blank canvas; on this canvas he deposits marks of paint; each mark modifies the look of the canvas; and when this process of modification has gone on long enough, the painter's work is at an end, and the surface of the canvas bears the finished picture" (Wollheim 1973a: 109).

Clearly this conception does not apply to the Reinhardt work, where the marks are "highly repetitive"; a monochrome work is only "minimally ahead of the tabula rasa which it supersedes" (*ibid.*). Hence, the traditional conception of engaging with (and appreciating) art will not apply. However, Wollheim goes on to say, constructing an image is only half of the story:

> [T]he image before us … is the result of the partial obliteration or simplifying of a more complex image that enjoyed some kind of shadowy pre-existence, and upon which the artist has gone to work. The "pre-image", as we might call it, was excessively differentiated, and the artist has dismantled it according to his own inner needs.
>
> (Wollheim 1973a: 110)

That is, appreciating the Reinhardt work is a matter of seeing it made in the traditional way, but as exhibiting "to an ultimate degree … the work of destruction". Most canvasses manifest the constructive phase of making; the Reinhardt work manifests the destructive phase. However, both of these phases are part of making a picture.

This attempt to find a continuity between traditional and radical works of art is only a partial success (and Wollheim claims no more than this). The principal difficulty is that there are many ways in which intentions can be successfully embodied in a work through the constructive phase, but few ways that intentions can be embodied in the destructive phase. In short, there are many ways in which a picture can manifest an image (I am not restricting this to a figurative image), but few ways (and at the limit, only one way) in which a picture can manifest the absence of an image. It might be that what is interesting about the destructive phase in a Reinhardt canvas is different from what is interesting about the destructive phase in another, but the viewer will not be able to access that by attending to the canvas. Once again, he or she will need either to access the artist's intentions directly, or have recourse to the network of relations between that canvas and the art theory and art history of the time.

***

We have returned to the issue left hanging at the end of Chapter 1. To what extent was there a decisive break with the past in the early twentieth century? That is, is the modernist concept of art distinct from our concept of fine art, and, if so, what is it? We could argue that there was a decisive break; the reasons why something is art, and the ways in which we engage with something as art, changed radically from the modern to the modernist era. However, this raises questions about the viability of the primary meaning of modernist work and, more radically, questions about the point and purpose of modernist art. The alternative is to argue that here was no decisive break: to find continuities in both the making and the appreciation of art. This would give modernist art a rationale – the same rationale as the art that came before – although this raises the question of how much of what has figured in the art world since Duchamp really can be considered as continuous with pre-Duchampian art, and what to do with the work that cannot be so considered.

6. BEAUTY AND UGLINESS

Francis Bacon's *Three Studies for Figures at the Base of a Crucifixion*

There are many different ways of doing philosophy. One way, which will be familiar from previous chapters, is to take a word in common parlance (say, "art") and try to give a precise statement of its meaning. A problem arises if common parlance does not use the word in a particularly systematic manner. If our use of the word is very loose, possibly even contradictory, then any precise statement of its meaning is either going to be a suggestion for tightening up the use or is going to be an inaccurate statement of what, in common parlance, the word means. That was the case, as we saw, with "art"; it is also the case with "beauty".

The question of the value of works of art is one we have returned to frequently in the course of this book. One value can be summed up in the term "beautiful"; a work is valuable to the extent that it is beautiful. However, as we saw in Chapter 2, this raises more questions than it settles. If being beautiful is merely a matter of eliciting pleasurable feelings, then being beautiful cannot be the same as being valuable. A work can elicit pleasurable feelings without our taking it to be valuable, and we can take a work to be valuable without it eliciting pleasurable feelings. However, there does seem to be *some* connection between art and beauty. What I shall try to do in this chapter is to say something illuminating about that connection.

The word "beautiful" is used in so many ways in ordinary language that we need to make a few distinctions before we can make anything clear. The obvious place to begin is with the thought that to be beautiful is to exhibit a pleasing appearance. We can divide the world into those things that are beautiful (roses and Donatello's *St George*); those things that are ugly (piles of rubbish and Oliver Cromwell); and those things (most things) falling somewhere in between. In this case, the beautiful contrasts with the ugly. We also use the word "beautiful" to make a contrast *within* those things that present a pleasing appearance. That is, we contrast things that are beautiful with things that *merely* present a pleasing appearance; perhaps we would call the latter sort of appearance "pretty". It is difficult to say what this contrast is. Perhaps being pretty is *merely* presenting a pleasing appearance while being beautiful is presenting an appearance that is not only pleasing, but interesting, arresting or in some other way valuable.

The category of things that present a pleasing appearance (whether or not they are also valuable) will include many works of art. Our second contrast also appears with respect to art: we use the word "beautiful" to draw a distinction between works that are valuable and works that are merely pretty. Matthew Kieran has said of "some of Renoir's lesser portraits" that they are "not far off the awful chocolate box pictures or birthday cards one often sees in gift shops" (Kieran 2005: 92). These pictures (we might say) are not beautiful, but rather are merely pretty.

Beauty, then, is not merely the presentation of a pleasing appearance but an appearance that is in some way valuable. One might try to specify the way in which a beautiful appearance was valuable. One might, for example, say with Francis Bacon (the seventeenth-century writer, not to be confused with the twentieth-century painter we shall be considering shortly) that "There is no excellent beauty that hath not some strangeness in the proportion" (Bacon [1607] 1931). An appearance with no such strangeness (e.g. an appearance that exhibits pure symmetry) would be merely pretty; an appearance with some quirk or strangeness might be beautiful. To embark on such a project would be to embark on an endless quest. The grounds for experiencing a pleasing appearance as valuable are many and varied. Similarly, the grounds for experiencing a pleasing appearance as not being valuable will also be many and varied. One might truly value the pleasing appearance of Bronzino's *Portrait of Lucrezia Panciatichi*, not only because of its visual delight and its high degree of skill, but also because of the impressive way in which the sitter's psychology has been made manifest in her face. In contrast, Kieran clearly finds his experience of some of Renoir's portraits vitiated by their sentimentality.

There are works of art where the pleasing appearance itself is a ground for valuing the work. Almost any painting by Bronzino, for example, possesses a feature, a kind of luminous appearance, that seems perfectly captured by saying that it is beautiful. This is a feature of the work on a par with other features of works such as being dynamic, balanced or unified, except that "beauty", unlike these, not only describes a work but praises it. In these cases, "beauty" seems to describe and commend a certain valuable feature.

Having separated the beautiful from the merely pretty, are we able to claim that all works of art are beautiful? Notoriously we are not, as there are many works of art that do not present a pleasing appearance and hence do not present a valuable pleasing appearance. The standard examples of such works are the Isenheim altarpiece, which depicts a crucified Christ covered in leprous sores, and Picasso's *Les Demoiselles d'Avignon*, which depicts angular nudes with unattractive and, in two cases, mask-like faces. The manner in which we deal with these examples is in part a terminological issue. One could maintain that such works are indeed not beautiful, although the appearance they present is valuable for other reasons. Alternatively, one could maintain that the relevant issue is the presentation of a valuable appearance, whether or not it is visually pleasing, and use this as grounds for claiming that the works are beautiful. Those who adopt the latter approach sometimes talk of there being two concepts of beauty (Scruton 2009: 15–17). The first concept is the one we have been discussing: a pleasing appearance that is also valuable. The second concept covers objects that do not necessarily have a pleasing appearance, but which are nonetheless valuable.

As I said above, the ordinary language use of "beautiful" seems too unsystematic to legislate on whether there are one, two or even three concepts. However, the "two concept" solution does allow a certain flexibility in setting up the debate. To keep matters clear, I shall reserve the term "beautiful" for something that presents a pleasing appearance that is valuable. I shall use the term "aesthetic merit" for the second concept: something that, whether or not it is pleasing, presents a valuable appearance.

Before this becomes even vaguely adequate, and I am not sure I shall be able to make it any more than vaguely adequate, I need to make two further distinctions. We need to distinguish between three senses of "valuable appearance". The first is that which interests me: where the value is found in the perceptual appearance of the object. Put in familiar terms, the appearance of the object repays attention for its own sake. However, there are other senses of "valuable appearance". Wellington no doubt found General Blücher's late appearance at the Battle of Waterloo valuable; in that sense, it was "a valuable appearance". Beauty, however, is linked not to the value of *making an appearance* but to the value of an exhibited appearance. Whether or not Blücher's turning up was valuable entails nothing about whether the appearance he exhibited (indeed, that of a rather stern Prussian) was valuable. I also do not mean "a valuable appearance" in the sense of "an appearance of something that is valuable". Money might present a valuable appearance in this sense, but it is easily distinguished from the sense we mean.

A more difficult issue is to substantiate my claim to have distinguished the beautiful from the pretty. I claimed that, at least according to the first concept, being beautiful was different from being pretty in that while both presented a pleasing appearance, only the former presented a valuable appearance. This appears to deny that prettiness is valuable, which seems absurd: it is surely more valuable for things to be pretty than not pretty. This raises some interesting questions, which we shall only be able to deal with in full below. For the moment, however, we should qualify our claim and concede that there is a continuum (at least in the first concept of the beautiful). There are pleasing appearances that are merely pleasing appearances and there are pleasing appearances that are more than this, being in some way more valuable or interesting. The term "pretty" usually describes the former, and the term "beautiful" the latter. Nothing in our first concept means we have to deny that the pretty entirely lacks value. The kinds of feature that move something along the scale from the merely pretty to the beautiful are whatever properties it is of the work that make the experience of it more substantially valuable.

There are, then, works of art that are merely pretty; works of art that are beautiful; and works of art that possess aesthetic merit. However, and this is the puzzle we shall consider for the rest of this chapter, sometimes a work's aesthetic merit can lie not in its beauty but in its ugliness. The example I shall use to introduce this puzzle is Francis Bacon's *Three Studies for Figures at the Base of a Crucifixion* (1944). These are three large paintings, each 94 cm × 74 cm. The background is a lurid orange colour. This is how they are described by Kieran:

> The viewer is presented by three separate canvases, reminiscent of a triptych, each depicting a strangely anthropomorphic animal-like form. The figure on the left is crouched on a table, huddling itself in a bird-like manner, its vaguely human face a quarter on and turned away. The central figure is side-on, the elongated neck stretching from the bulbous, ostrich-like body, bringing its face in full confrontation with the viewer. The threatening, repulsive, mouth of lips and teeth is somewhat agape, and where there should be eyes the face is bandaged. The mouth emerges directly from the neck rather than belonging to a distinct face. The third canvas represents a sharpened, cow-like body, its elongated neck bringing a viciously howling mouth into a three-quarter view. The neck opens up into rows of teeth, an ear placed behind the lower jaw just out, the mouth stretches open in a

scream, extended in a manner impossible for any human skull. These frightened, blind, raging figures are visceral in their impact, jolting one into sensations of fright, horror, isolation, and angst. Their force derives from the fusion of bestial forms with anthropomorphising faces. We react to them as self-conscious creatures, their postures and expressions revealing feelings of petrified isolation, searing horror, pain and blind confusion. But the heads, though recognisably akin to human faces, are distinctly anything other than human. The painful emotions we feel in response to them are shot through with the recognition that these creatures both are and are not akin to ourselves. In a profound sense they both portray and threaten our conceptions of what it is like to be an embodied human being. For here are creatures, ugly, deformed, who suffer deeply in their self-conscious condition, and yet are radically removed from something we would recognisably call human.   (Kieran 2005: 185)

The appearance of these three paintings is not pretty. It is also not beautiful in the sense specified above: it is does not present a pleasing visual appearance. It is, however, an astonishing work; it certainly possesses aesthetic merit. This raises two questions that I shall deal with in the rest of this chapter. The first is a question about the motivations of the viewers. Why would anyone want to look at a work that presents such a horrible appearance? The second is about the motivations of the painter, and also about the value of the painting. Why would anyone want to paint such horrible pictures? Are the pictures valuable despite their horrible appearance, or because of their horrible appearance?

The first of these questions is a version of what is sometimes known as "the paradox of tragedy". David Hume poses the problem as follows:

It seems an unaccountable pleasure which the spectators of a well-written tragedy receive from sorrow, terror, anxiety, and other passions that are in themselves disagreeable and uneasy. The more they are touched and affected, the more are they delighted with the spectacle; and as soon as the uneasy passions cease to operate, the piece is at an end.   (Hume [1757] 1993c: 126)

As Kieran says, the figures "both portray and threaten our conceptions of what it is like to be an embodied human being". That sounds an unpleasant state to be in, so why would anyone voluntarily put themselves into that state?

It is easy to understand why one would want to look at a beautiful painting; as we have seen, the beauty of a painting is a value. Why, however, would anyone actively find, and gaze at, such horrors?

Here is one attempt at explanation. The reason people go on holiday, despite having to queue at airports, is that the irritations of queuing are outweighed by other benefits such as experiencing far-off places. Analogously, one might argue that the triptych has various valuable features, such as the skill of the painting and the intensity of Bacon's vision, which outweigh the unpleasantness of regarding the figures. This seems to me a poor explanation. If queuing is vexatious, then the holiday would have been better if we did not have to queue. Put another way, the holiday was valuable *despite* our having to queue. However, the same is not true of the triptych. It would be absurd to claim that the pictures would have been better had the figures not been so gruesome. It is not that the picture is valuable *despite* the figures being gruesome; it is valuable *because* the figures are gruesome. I shall consider a more sophisticated version of this explanation below.

A second attempt at explanation fares equally badly, at least when it comes to great art. It is a fact about people that they tend to be fascinated by horror; people slow down to look at the carnage following a car accident. If we generalize this psychological truth to our case, the claim would be that people look at the triptych to satisfy their fascination with the grotesque. It strikes me as plausible that this might explain an audience's engagement with some horrific appearances: schlock horror films, for example. Directors attempt to outdo each other in blood, guts and gore. (The best guide to the genre is Joe Bob Briggs, here on *Escape 2000*: "Twenty-one breasts, including two stunt breasts. Thirty-four dead bodies. Six pints of blood. One beast [gonzo werewolf]. Four motor vehicle chases, two crash-and-burns. Heads roll. Hands roll. Stomachs roll. Little toe rolls. Three stars. Joe Bob says check this baby out" [1989: 210].) The problem with this purported explanation is that it would be impossible to explain the value of *great* art that was not beautiful. The value of grindhouse films is largely that they pander to our voyeurism of the horrific. In other words, their value is in feeding desires we do not regard as particularly valuable; we might even think such desires regrettable. Unless we think works such as Bacon's triptych are only as valuable as grindhouse films, and for the same reason, we shall have to reject this explanation.

The best way to approach this problem is not to solve it as much as to dissolve it. The problem gets a grip on us by presenting us with a contrast. On the one side we have a beautiful appearance, which we regard with pleasure. On the other side, we have a horrible appearance, which we regard with the opposite of pleasure (something like pain). On the plausible assumption that we are motivated to pursue pleasures and not pains, it becomes difficult to see why we would seek to regard horrible appearances.

The contrast, however, is incomplete as it omits any mention of *value*. If an experience were valuable, that would provide us with a motivation to undergo it. What if there were some horrible appearances that we regard with pain, which we nonetheless considered valuable? If so, we could have a more sophisticated version of the first explanation we dismissed above. Our experience of the gruesomeness of the figures has two features: it is unpleasant and it is valuable. The reason I am willing to experience the picture is because its unpleasantness (which derives from its gruesomeness) is outweighed by its value (which also derives from its gruesomeness). We cannot condemn this version of the explanation for holding that the figures are valuable *despite* their being gruesome; it is explicit that they are valuable *because* they are gruesome.

If we allow that unpleasant experiences can be valuable (a question I shall consider below), then this explanation seems viable. We might, however, question whether its description of looking at the triptych is correct. This explanation maintains that the experience of the gruesome figures really is unpleasant: an unpleasantness being outweighed by the value of the experience. Is the experience of being caught up in looking at the triptych, being overwhelmed by its form and content, really *unpleasant*? It is worth thinking a little more about the role of pleasure. It is true that beautiful appearances are usually regarded with pleasure. However, it does not follow that, of all appearances, *only* beautiful ones are regarded with pleasure. We can take pleasure in ugly appearances that are, for other reasons, interesting or compelling (Budd 1995: 117). It is difficult to say precisely what pleasure is to be found in contemplating Bacon's painting. In claiming that we experience it with pleasure, I do not mean to say anything inconsistent with Keiran's characterization above. That is, our experience of the work is characterized by the negative emotions of pain and disgust. The claim is rather that such experiences are consistent with our taking pleasure in the work. If we take her "beautiful" to refer to what I have above called "aesthetic merit", we can agree with Mary Mothersill, who noted that "pleasure in the beautiful is multi-hued and may be tinged with awe and melancholy as with gaiety and exhilaration" (Mothersill 1986: 272). Whether we want to maintain that the experience is pleasant or unpleasant (with the pleasantness being a rather peculiar, stretched, sort), our being motivated to experience an appearance that is not beautiful is not itself puzzling. We are motivated by the experience being a valuable experience, which either outweighs the unpleasantness of the experience, or is itself a pleasure of a sort.

I claimed above that the problem with explaining our motivation to experience works such as Bacon's triptych as a fascination with horror is that it fails to explain the value we find in such works. Even if we concede the argument I have just given, and grant that there is a respectable pleasure to be had in the contemplation of interesting or compelling appearances that are nonetheless horrible, we do not yet have an account of the value of such experiences. This brings us on to our second question: what could motivate someone to produce a work such as the one we are considering? What aesthetic merit could there be in such ugliness? Throughout this book I have stressed the point that the sources of the non-instrumental value of our experiences of works are many and various, and the same is true here. There will be no one explanation of why works that exhibit ugly appearances are valuable and hence no one explanation of why an artist should embark on the kind of project on which Bacon embarked (Budd 1995: 117). Having said that, some think it is no accident that the post-war avant-garde has been involved in a flight from beauty; it is the only possible response to the horrors manifest in the world in the mid-twentieth century.

In the Introduction, I drew an analogy between the way the history of art develops and the way a conversation develops. As we have seen, there are some ways in which the argument can be overstated. It can, however, help us to make sense of the point being made here. Somehow, there came a point in time when artists (or, rather, some artists) felt that they could no longer continue producing figurative work. In 1959, looking back to the 1930s, Rothko said "it was with the utmost reluctance that I found the figure could not suit my purposes ... But a time came when none of us could use the figure without mutilating it" (quoted in Anfam 1990: 81). There is something curious about this: why did artists in the mid-twentieth century find that they could not paint a figure "without mutilating it"? What was so tricky about painting a figure? The answer suggested by the analogy with conversation is that the topic had moved on; it was no longer a time when figures *could* be painted. As I argued earlier, in some ways this is an exaggeration. One can pick a history of development out of the history of art, but only by a process of selection that suits the story one wants to tell. There were artists apart from Rothko, such as Freud and Bacon, who did not have similar anxieties about painting a figure. However, such anxieties about painting, as we have seen, did play a large part in the visual arts of the twentieth century and beyond. By looking at this we are able to get one view – a view associated with the work of the philosopher Theodor Adorno – as to the value of ugliness in the visual arts.

Matisse wrote, in 1908:

> What I dream of is an art of balance, of purity and serenity, devoid of troubling or depressing subject matter, an art which could be for every mental worker, for the businessman as well as the man of letters, for example, a soothing, calming influence on the mind, something like a good armchair which provides relaxation from physical fatigue.   (Matisse [1908] 1993: 76)

This is one view that, because it comes from an artist as great as Matisse, cannot be gainsaid. On this view, however, Bacon's painting would make no sense because it is hardly "devoid of troubling or depressing subject matter". This raises a question we have touched on several times in the book already: what is the role of art? What is it for? In Chapter 2 we looked at what we might find valuable about a particular work of art, but what, more generally, is the function of art?

If the function of art were merely decoration (which is one way we might read the quotation from Matisse above) then it would be difficult to make sense of difficult and troubling art. However, we have seen that art is *not* merely decoration: some artists (at least) are trying to produce something of more than merely decorative value; they are trying to *say* something. The question, then, is what function does art have that allows artists to say something by producing difficult and troubling art? The question is ill formed, of course, because there is no reason to suppose that art has only one function. However, one prominent function art has had that does enable artists to say something about the human situation is that of mediating between human beings and the world. Human beings are self-conscious animals. We find ourselves thrown into a world that is (generally) not of our making. Worse, that world can sometimes seem a difficult and inhospitable place. Fate is capricious; those things on which we rely can be snatched away from us, and justice seems an ideal that is seldom realized. We turn to systems of thought to try to make sense of this: religious faith, art and, perhaps, philosophy.

In an essay that condenses a remarkable amount of learning into a small number of pages, Raymond Geuss has argued that one of the influences of art for the nineteenth-century German philosopher Friedrich Hegel was for it to be part of a "theodicy": the project of showing that the world "is basically rational, good, and commensurate to us" (Geuss 1999: 83). Throughout the ages, art has attempted to embody the ideas of the time (the German term for this is "the zeitgeist", which has slipped into common usage). In pre-classical times, the "Symbolic period", ideas were unformed and indeterminate. Thus, ideas could not correspond to concrete things, and hence the art of that time tends to be symbolic. Objects are symbols for abstractions, such as a lion becoming a symbol for strength. Classical times fare much better: "it is the free and adequate embodiment of the Idea in the shape peculiarly appropriate to the Idea itself in its essential nature", as Hegel said ([1842] 1979). Roughly, the classical period had a determinate idea of the divine: namely, idealized persons. The art of the classical period – sculpture – is uniquely well suited to expressing such an idea, resulting in the classical statues of idealized forms. In the third period, the Romantic period, the idea that needs to be expressed is that of the Christian God: a determinate idea of an indeterminate thing. This is an idea that art is barely able to express, and Hegel is forced to the rather desperate measure of claiming that painting, music and poetry are the ideal art forms for the period in as much as they embody abstraction in something concrete (*ibid.*: 76–87).

In much the same way as modernist theory attempted to draw on art history for support, Hegel's philosophy drew on art history, albeit from a much wider historical period (this is no accident, in that modernism reflected the Hegelian roots of much thinking about the arts). At each period, the arts embodied the ideas that would best mediate between humanity and the world in which it found itself. The terrible jolt that art receives in the modern period is that it becomes increasingly difficult to believe that the world *is* basically "rational, good, and commensurate to us". The reasons for this decline in optimism are many and varied, but we could begin a plausible list. There is the decline of religion and its replacement by a rather alienating naturalism; a rise in aspirations that are frequently thwarted; a series of events in which people behave appallingly towards other people, including genocidal attacks on whole populations; the general awful banality of modern social arrangements; and the fact that all this bad news is brought, by modern means of communication, into our living rooms. Faced with all this, if an artist is trying to say something about the world, it is not to be marvelled at that he or she is drawn away from presenting pleasing and consoling appearances.

Whatever the merits of this argument, it should not be confused with the simple thought that to truly represent an ugly world art itself must be ugly. Titian's *The Rape of Lucretia* (1568–71) represents an ugly scene but is not itself ugly. Rather, the defence of ugly works of art that is being offered is that we have to admit that theodicy has failed: the world cannot be saved by appearances. Art ought not to console; if the artist wants to say something truthful about the world, he or she needs to cease to present it through the lens of the beautiful. Even with this caveat, our argument still has not taken us very far to an understanding of works such as Bacon's painting. Let us grant that, for the reasons given, it is an evasion to prettify the world. However, the *Three Studies for Figures at the Base of a Crucifixion* does not merely seek to portray ugliness as it really is. That is, it is not simply a faithful depiction of dreadful scenarios or ugly events. Rather, inasmuch as the painting does convey "searing horror" (to use Kieran's term) it does so not so much in the scene it depicts, but in the manner in which it depicts it. It seems that here Bacon agrees with Rothko: "none of us could use the figure without mutilating it".

Here we need to recall the discussion from Chapter 1, picked up again when we looked at Richter's work in Chapter 4. It is part of the modernist concept of art that painting cannot simply go on as it did before. Danto attempts to provide an account of the content of art that draws on its relations with the art theory around at the time the work was produced. Richter, as we saw, attempted to give painting life by drawing on some of the features of photographs. Bacon faces the same problem; the conversation has moved on. He cannot attempt to capture horror in the same manner as Goya (for example) captured horror; he would simply end up producing works that would be understood as being painted in the eighteenth-century style. Hence, he is working with various constraints: he wants to express the bleakness of the world, and he needs to find a way of doing so that is not going to look stylistically reactionary. Once one starts to appreciate his problem, one can start to appreciate the quality of his solution. In particular, one can appreciate that the absence of beauty in the picture calls for no special explanation.

There is, then, no special problem with ugly works of art. Bacon's triptych can be seen as a response to a world that demands a howl of pain. That something is ugly does not imply that it lacks aesthetic merit, any more than that something presents a pleasing appearance implies that it possesses aesthetic merit. I suggested above that the existence of ugly works of art raised two questions: why would anyone want to look at such works; and why would anyone want to produce such works? I have argued that both questions rest on a misunderstanding: that what we see in art, and what gives value to art, is beauty (in the sense of "presenting a pleasing appearance"). Beauty, in this sense, is a source of value: sometimes a great source of value. However, it is not the only source of value; there are many more besides. Furthermore, these latter values – as they show up in our experience of works of art – can be experienced with pleasure, albeit of a rather stretched sort.

7. ART AND KNOWLEDGE

Edward Hopper's *Nighthawks*

When I discussed the value of art in Chapter 2, I put forward the idea that the value of art lies, at least in part, in the knowledge it conveys. I rejected the view – at least in its simple form – on the grounds that conveying such knowledge would be an instrumental value and the value of art (when considered as art) is non-instrumental. The reason for returning to this question is because a puzzle remains. There are reasons for thinking that engaging with art exercises not only our sensations and our feelings, but also our cognitive selves: art broadens the mind. Walking around a gallery is hard work; engaging with paintings can be exhilarating, but it is also tiring. Furthermore, we sometimes feel as if we have understood something. Spending time among paintings by masters such as Rembrandt or Turner seems to *teach* us things. However, what it teaches us often remains elusive. We could gesture at it: it teaches us something about mortality, perhaps. However, once we press harder and ask for specifics – what do we know now that we did not know before? – we are hard-pressed to give an answer. Hence, there is a question prior to that of whether teaching us is part of the value of art; we need to sort out whether art is able to teach us at all (Gaut 2003: 436).

I shall begin by putting some issues to one side. There are many things we can learn when we turn our eyes to the gallery wall. Using our eyes is a reliable way of finding out all kinds of things about our environment: that we are in a gallery; that we are faced with pictures; that this particular gallery has pictures by Rembrandt in it; and so on. All this is uncontroversial; it is news to nobody that we use our eyes to acquire beliefs about our environment. The topic in this chapter is a more specific claim. Let us start with the issue of whether we can learn things from the content of a work of art.

The example I shall discuss is one of the best-known pieces of American realist art: Edward Hopper's *Nighthawks* (1942). The picture is fairly large – 84 cm × 153 cm – and very arresting. It depicts a late night coffee bar with three customers and a counterman. We look through the windows of the bar, which curve around a corner. It is night outside, and the bar is fully lit by a harsh light. As is the case in many of Hopper's pictures, the individuals seem lost in solipsistic isolation; nobody's gaze meets that of anyone else. The colours are all fairly muted, as they would be at night. The choice of colour, the shadows, the emptiness of the street, make the painting strongly reminiscent of early paintings by Giorgio de Chirico in addition to the more obvious echoes of other American realists such as Norman Rockwell.

Our question is whether engaging with *Nighthawks* can give us knowledge. *Prima facie*, it seems as if it can. It does seem to capture something, whether that be that cities alienate people from each other or that bars (coffee or otherwise) are refuges from the dark world outside, conforming to Hemingway's description of "a clean well-lighted place". The world of *Nighthawks* seems akin to the world captured by other of Hemingway's short stories (one of which – "The Killers" – might have inspired the picture). We could sum it up rather weakly as something in the area of the existential loneliness characteristic of modern living.

The difficulty of saying exactly what it is that *Nighthawks* might teach us nicely captures the claim of those who believe that we cannot acquire knowledge from the content of art. The anti-cognitivist argument is given in a paper by Jerome Stolnitz, tellingly entitled "On the Cognitive Triviality of Art" (1992). Stolnitz's principal point is that there is no such thing as "artistic knowledge" as there is "scientific knowledge" or "religious knowledge". Along the way, he makes the point that if we try to capture what it is that works of art teach us, we generally end up with the staggeringly banal. His example is *Pride and Prejudice*, which would, he says, teach us that "stubborn pride and ignorant prejudice keep attractive people apart" (Stolnitz 1992: 193). As Stolnitz says, as a cognitive achievement that is "skimpy" and likely to be something any reader of the novel would already know, hence not some item of knowledge the novel could teach. The same point could be made about our example. What does it purport to teach us: that in the city at night, people can get lonely? If not that, what? Any attempt to put the "message" of the work into words seems, as we have seen, to reduce it to the level of the words of wisdom found in a cracker.

The attack on art as a source of knowledge has a distinguished pedigree. In Plato's description of his ideal society in the *Republic*, the poets are banned.

One line of argument that runs throughout Book X of that work is that the nature of poetry pulls it away from truth (I shall generalize Plato's arguments from poetry to the visual arts). To illustrate this Plato presents us with a case that contrasts a proper skill, the making of bridles, with the arts. The cobbler and the smith make the bridle but even they do not know (at least initially) what makes a good bridle. The person who does know is the horseman because he will know whether what he has been given is or is not performing its function efficiently. The horseman will then be able to tell the cobbler and the smith what works well and what does not, so they can improve their design accordingly. This feedback from user to maker can continue until the horseman has a bridle that properly performs its function. The same is true of other skills. Consider, for example, the skill of being a general. Whether someone possesses the skills of generalship is shown in battle. If he does possess the skills he will survive as a general; if he does not, then he will not. The products of skills are tested in use and (should people survive this use) they will be able to pass the information back to the "maker". It is part of what it is to be a skill that there is this orientation towards getting things right (*Republic* 601c–e).

The arts, however, are not like this. For a work of art to be successful it needs to appeal as a work of art. In other words, works of art succeed to the extent that they appeal to their audience. However, there is no link between the features that make a work appealing and truth. The features that make a film appealing might be the indestructibility of the hero, the flawless beauty of the protagonists and the inevitable fall of the villain. The appeal of such features is no guide as to whether it is true that heroes are indestructible, that there are flawlessly beautiful people or that villains inevitably get their just deserts. Of course, these things *may* be true; it is only that featuring in a successful work of art is no guide to whether or not they *are* true. In essence, the function of the content of the work of art is to appeal; success at being appealing is independent of truth. There is no link between the content of a work of art and truth. Of course, the content might be true and, if it is, it might teach us true things. However, for art to count as a source of *knowledge* it has to be more than simply accidentally true. If someone simply guessed what the weather was going to be like tomorrow, and they turned out to be right, we would not say that they *knew* what the weather was going to be like tomorrow. Unless it was more than an accident that art was right when it was right, it cannot be a source of knowledge. If Plato's arguments are correct, then art can never be more than accidentally right, and therefore cannot be a source of knowledge.

Let us return to our example. First, there is no reason to think that there was any such diner, inhabited by any such people, on any such empty street. However, this need not trouble the cognitivist because these are not the kinds of knowledge Hopper's painting was meant to convey. Rather, they were truths of greater import, such as that urban living is alienating. Let us grant that this is indeed the "message" of the work. Plato's question is why we have any reason to believe it. Hopper wanted to paint a successful picture and he did it by painting a particularly arresting scene. There is no reason for us to think that any propositions expressed by that picture are true.

We can compare *Nighthawks* with a picture that does convey knowledge, for example a sketch of the defendant by a courtroom artist. Let us say the courtroom sketch depicts the defendant as wearing a spotty dress. On seeing the picture, it would be reasonable for us to believe that the defendant wore a spotty dress. However, it would not be reasonable to believe that on the basis of the picture alone. We need information from outside the picture. That is, we need to know that what we are looking at is a courtroom sketch and that courtroom sketches are reliable. If we grant that such external information is needed for our forming the belief to be reasonable, then it does not look as if *Nighthawks* and the courtroom sketch stand in such a marked contrast. If we had external information about *Nighthawks* (e.g. that Hopper wished to convey a truth for which he had amassed considerable evidence) then it too could be a reliable source of information. In other words, the fact that something is a work of art is not the relevant issue in deciding whether or not it is a source of knowledge. What we have, rather, is a general truth about *all* representations, whether they are works of art or not. Our using them as a basis for belief will be justified only if they are reliable. Whether or not they are reliable is something we could not learn from the representation itself; it is something we would need to learn about the representation.

This reply does not, I think, meet Plato's challenge. Plato's worry was that art has a certain function – to be appealing – and that this function has no connection with truth. The function of a courtroom sketch is to be a reliable source of information and this does have a connection with truth. It is true that we need external information to know what it is that we are looking at. Nonetheless, once we know something is a work of art, and it is functioning as a work of art, we have no reason to think that the world is as it represents the world to be.

Is Plato correct? Is there an insuperable problem with art conveying knowledge? Before we concede to Plato it is worth noticing that, so far, we have been using a rather narrow concept of knowledge: that is, the acquisition of new beliefs from a reliable source. Even if Plato were right about this, art might be able to enable other sorts of cognitive achievement. I shall consider three.

In finding our way around the world, we rely on our beliefs. If I want to buy some coffee and I believe my local delicatessen sells coffee, then I go to my local delicatessen. If I need some money and I believe the nearest ATM is just around the corner, then I go just around the corner. That much is relatively simple. However, our actual psychologies are a little bit messier. I might not want to pay a big library fine and believe that the only way of avoiding paying a big library fine is by taking my book back to the library, but still not take my book back to the library (I just can't face it). More dramatically, most if not all of us would like there to be less suffering in the world and believe that there are all sort of things we could do to alleviate suffering, and yet still not act so as to alleviate suffering. We might simply be paralysed by the amount of suffering there is, and feel that what we could do would be a mere drop in the ocean. It is not simply that we have various beliefs and act on them; it is rather that the beliefs have different "weights" for us. A news report might not give us any new beliefs (we knew all along that there was a famine in the Horn of Africa) but it might make a belief more salient. Confronted with images of our fellow human beings in terrible circumstances, the belief that there is a famine in the Horn of Africa might weigh more heavily with us and move us to make a donation to charity.

Rather than giving us new beliefs, then, art might change the salience of the beliefs that we have. Rosalind Hursthouse has described a nice example that illustrates the case.

> I was lucky enough to get to Madrid and see both Goya's paintings on war and Picasso's *Guernica* … It created in me an image of "war as terrible" which is dominatingly vivid. Now, when I look at pictures which represent war as glorious, or read poems, novels or plays about military glory, or honour and courage displayed in war, or see films about them, or hear music supposed to invoke a passionate willingness to fight for one's country or one's cause, Goya's and Picasso's paintings always come into my thoughts. "No, no," they always say, "don't be fooled. *This* the way it is – terrible, terrible."
>
> (Hursthouse 1992: 278–9)

Nighthawks might have an effect of the same kind. It does not purport to give us any new information but it does make some information more salient. Thoughts of alienation and the possibility of ennui dominate our minds, and might persuade us to spend more time building our relationships so as to avoid loneliness in later life (Hopper's romanticizing of loneliness will be discussed below).

I have no doubt that the phenomenon Hursthouse is describing is real. The power of art to make some thoughts salient makes it a powerful means of conveying political messages. However, the shift from acquiring new beliefs to reorganizing the salience of our old beliefs does not provide a way of escaping Plato's scepticism for exactly the same problem occurs in the new case: are our beliefs being reorganized in a way that matches the way the world is or are they being reorganized in a distorted way? Hursthouse's own case provides a good illustration. She left Madrid with the horror of war dominating her thoughts. How do we know that is the right way to think about war? After all, all she has seen are some powerful pictures on the matter. Who is to say that were she to have seen some other pictures (e.g. George William Joy's *General Gordon's Last Stand* [1894]), her mind might not have been moved in a different direction. If Plato is right and art is an unreliable source for beliefs, it is equally unreliable as a means for changing the salience of our beliefs.

Hursthouse's point takes us into the murky world of how to think about morality. It contrasts the standard view of acquiring moral knowledge (getting new beliefs) with a more subtle view (rebalancing our existing beliefs). Discussing the second sort of cognitive achievement art might facilitate takes us further down this road. Consider the parody of the way an upright moral character behaves. I call this "a parody" because it is not clear that it describes any actual behaviour, although it does describe one end of a spectrum. A moral person is one who goes around armed with a number of general moral rules: the good should be maximized, evil should not go unpunished, moral people are worthy of respect, and so on. They are then able to bring instances they encounter under these rules. When they have a chance to, they maximize the good; when they find evil, they attempt to have it punished; when they encounter a moral person, they accord that person respect. Acquiring moral knowledge is a matter of learning these rules. Hence, if we are to prove the claim that art can impart moral knowledge, we would have to prove that art is a reliable source of information concerning moral rules. This looks an easy target from both sources of scepticism described above. Stolnitz would argue that art could never teach us anything but trivialities and Plato would argue that art could not be a reliable teacher even of those.

There are other models of acquiring moral knowledge apart from the learning of rules, however. Consider how someone might come to value domesticity. As a young person, their heads are full of tales of adventure and derring-do, the heroics of conquest and Henry V at Agincourt. They are scornful of a life spent building a home and cultivating a garden. How might they come to value this latter way of life? It is unlikely to come about by learning the rule "domesticity and cultivating one's garden have merit as a way of life". There is an alternative model of moral knowledge, however, that goes back at least as far as Aristotle. It has been developed in relation to art (specifically to literature) by Martha Nussbaum, who sums it up as follows: "in good deliberation and judgement, the particular is in some sense prior to general rules and principles" (1990c: 165). That is, if our young person experiences some particular people building a home, and finding worth in living that kind of life, he or she might come to see the value in it.

Consider another example. There is a perennial danger in life of being seduced by surface charm and attractiveness. In such a state, one can either neglect to worry about whether there is anything beneath the surface, or convince oneself that the superficially vapid is in fact quite profound. On the first model of moral knowledge, one could avoid this by learning the rule "Never marry an airhead". However, the rule itself will not be much use. How would one spot an airhead, especially if one is already seduced by his or her surface charm and attractiveness? Furthermore, airheadedness comes in degrees; one might think it worth trading some degree of airheadedness for a great deal of surface charm and attractiveness. If, instead of merely ingesting the rule, one focuses on a particular case of someone who has married an airhead, of vicariously experiencing the attraction, of witnessing the consequences, and experiences the situation with all its subtle nuances and fine discriminations, one may end up with the right kind of knowledge. Having focused on and learned from the particular situation, one has grasped the full import of the injunction not to marry an airhead in a useful form.

The problem, however, is in experiencing a situation "with all its subtle nuances, and fine discriminations". This is not often given to us in life. Furthermore, even if we come across some such situation, we cannot always get behind the eyes of the protagonists to know what they see or how they feel. This, according to Nussbaum, is where great art comes to our aid. Works of art present such situations to us in a much particularized way. Artists can tell us, or show us, how people see the world and how they experience situations. As she puts it, there is in much literature:

> a sustained exploration of particular lives … it is, in fact, not possible
> to speak about the moral view revealed in this text without speaking

at the same time of the created text, which exemplifies and expresses the responses of an imagination that means to care for, and to put itself there for us.   (Nussbaum 1990b: 139–41)

To return to our example, experiencing the marriage of Dr Lydgate and Rosamond Vincy through reading George Eliot's *Middlemarch* will teach you more about not marrying an airhead than will any book of moral philosophy or marriage guidance. Furthermore, Nussbaum is able to answer Stolnitz's charge of triviality. Certainly, ripped from its particular context and stated as a general truth ("Don't marry an airhead"), the knowledge looks trivial. However, Nussbaum's point is that it cannot be ripped from its context; it is not possible to separate the moral view from the created text. It is only by "living through" the situation that we grasp what the book is making available to us. What Nussbaum says about literature can transfer to the visual arts. Pieter de Hooch's picture *The Courtyard of a House in Delft* (1658) is an image of the modest virtues of domesticity. To engage with the picture is to understand these virtues and how they could be valuable.

The sceptic, however, will have the same reply as before. Even if Plato were to grant that experiencing the particular did teach us something and that works of art were a good, perhaps the only, way of experiencing particulars in the right kind of way (as fully realized, with all the subtle nuances and fine discriminations intact) that would not show that what we were taught was knowledge. De Hooch's picture is rhetorically in favour of the modest virtues of domesticity, but what reason do we have for thinking this reliable? What reason do we have for thinking *Middlemarch* a good guide to relationships? For all the reasons given above, we have no reason to think that what we learn from the content of works of art is true.

The last of the three sorts of cognitive achievement I shall consider relies less on works of art teaching us things, but on our using works of art as an aid to our own reasoning in a way that might affect our values. With respect to the acquisition of factual knowledge, Gregory Currie is sympathetic to the sceptics. He holds that we can acquire factual knowledge from fiction, but only by carefully distinguishing what is fictional from the background knowledge of fact. However, Currie argues that we use our imagination when we engage with fiction, which can bring about changes in our values and in the degree with which we are in tune with our values (Currie 1995: 255).

Currie presents what has become a standard model of engaging with fiction: "When I engage with fiction I simulate the process of acquiring beliefs – the beliefs I would acquire if I took the work I am engaged with for fact rather than fiction" (*ibid.*: 256). In Raymond Chandler's *Farewell, My Lovely*, Philip Marlowe reports, "I needed a drink, I needed a lot of life insurance, I needed a vacation, I needed a home in the country". When I read that, I do not *believe* that Marlowe needed such things, but I *imagine* that he needed such things. Currie calls this "primary imagining", which – clearly – does not give us knowledge about Marlowe's needs for, Marlowe being fictional, there is no such knowledge to be had. However, in addition to primary imagining, reading also involves what Currie calls "secondary imagining": readers also need to "imagine various things *so as to* imagine what is fictional" (*ibid.*).

Let us consider an example. At the end of Chandler's *The Big Sleep*, Marlowe faces a moral dilemma: whether or not to go to the police with information that he has. Readers imagine certain propositions such as "Marlowe knows Carmen Sternwood shot Rusty Regan"; that is primary imagining. In order to engage with the book, we need to have some grasp of what is going through Marlowe's head; his "thoughts, anxieties, visual and auditory experiences and bodily sensations" (*ibid.*). Having a grasp of this provides some content for our primary imagining: namely, which propositions about Marlowe we are to imagine are true. That is, we will know whether to imagine Marlowe did not go to the police because he nurtured loving feelings for Carmen's sister, and so on. Secondary imagining involves our imaginatively putting ourselves in Marlowe's shoes and imagining the world from his perspective. It is the fact that the novel gets us to take on some other person's perspective, their particular problems and situations, that enables us to learn something about ourselves.

> If our imagining goes well, it will tell us something about how we would respond to the situation, and what it would be like to experience it: a response and a phenomenology we can then transfer to the character. That way we learn something about the character. More importantly from the point of view of moral knowledge, we learn something about ourselves and about the things we regard, or might regard, as putative values. (*Ibid.*: 257)

In secondary imaginings, we use our own reactions to model the character's reactions but, of course, we also learn about our own reactions. We imagine what it is like to be faced with a decision, and note what we find difficult or easy, acceptable or unacceptable, in thinking through that decision. In the process of so doing, as Currie says, we learn about what we value and thus can think about whether we value what we ought to value. Engaging with fictions can give us knowledge: knowledge of what we value.

Let us apply this to the example we are considering in this chapter. The exact nature of the relation between the imagination and our engaging with pictures is a matter of dispute. Let us assume that there is something analogous to Currie's "primary imagining": that, on looking at *Nighthawks*, we imagine that there are four people in a late-night coffee bar. Is there something analogous to "secondary imagining"? It seems that there is: we can imagine what the world is like from the perspective of one of those people. We can imagine life from the perspective of someone for whom there is nothing to do late at night except to sit alone in such a bar.

Such an activity is less vulnerable to Platonic scepticism. The work of art is aiming not to teach us anything, but rather to get us to rehearse in our imaginations various possible but not actual situations from the perspective of a protagonist. While it is less vulnerable to Platonic scepticism, it is not, however, immune. Currie sums up the contribution made by fiction (whether literary fiction or a painting) as follows:

> [I]t is often hard for us to sustain an imaginative exploration of a complex situation. That is where fiction comes in. Fictions can act as aids to the imagination – holding our attention, making a situation vivid for us, and generally drawing us along in the wake of the narrative. If they can help us to enter empathically into the characters, we can come to feel what it is like to be those characters, make their choices, pursue their goals, and reap the rewards and the costs of their actions.
> (Currie 1998: 163–4)

The content of the fiction structures our imaginative engagement with the work. This allows the sceptic to say that if the fiction is unreliable, what we imagine will not necessarily be what we would experience were we in those circumstances. Consider, for example, using a fiction to imagine what it would be like to profit by the proceeds of a crime. Our thoughts and affective reactions will be at least affected by whether the fiction depicts the wrongdoer as happy (as tends to be the case in "caper" movies) or wracked with guilt and remorse (as is the case in *Crime and Punishment*). The sceptic does not need to maintain that we will always go along with the sentiments of the narrative; when we engage with fiction, we do sometimes suspend our usual values. They need only maintain that the fiction can influence our imaginative project, which would be difficult for Currie to deny because that is the core of his theory. Because there is influence, and because fiction is unreliable, our imaginative project will be unreliable. Because the imaginative project is unreliable, any beliefs we form as a result of it will not be knowledge.

Each of the three ways I have described in which art might provide us with a measure of cognitive achievement is true of our engagement with some works of art at some times. As we have seen, each is vulnerable to the sceptic's charge that the works cannot provide us with knowledge. I do not think that the sceptical challenge can be answered completely; however, there are two things we can say to mitigate it.

First, as I said above in introducing Hursthouse's view, art need not give us new *beliefs* but rather alter our cognitive states in some other way. Hursthouse argued that art can change the salience our beliefs have for us: give them a different "weight". Nussbaum argued that moral philosophy should focus on particular cases. The advantage they have over general theories is that they can improve our moral sensibilities, making us (to quote again from Henry James and the title of one of Nussbaum's essays) "finely aware and richly responsible" (Nussbaum 1990c). That is, art does not teach us new beliefs, new moral rules to follow, but helps us to see the world differently: to see when people deserve respect, or see a situation as meriting action or a person as shallow and sentimental. Finally, Currie does not think our exercises of imagination provide us with knowledge of facts, but rather different patterns of behaviour. As he points out – and this applies also to Hursthouse and Nussbaum – this also serves as a reply to Stolnitz's concerns that, even if works of art can provide us with knowledge, that knowledge will be trivial.

> We need not think of this as a process by which we learn *facts* about what is right and good … We might instead see it as a process by which we learn to *behave* in various desirable ways; moral knowledge may be, in part, practical rather than theoretical knowledge. And if it is that kind of knowledge that we get from fiction, then we have an explanation for the seemingly rather embarrassing fact that it is nearly always impossible to state, without descending into triteness, what you learned from a fictional narrative. Just as my inability to offer you a theory of bicycle riding is no objection to the claim that I know how to ride a bicycle, so my inarticulateness in the face of the question "What did you learn from *Middlemarch*?" is no refutation of the claim that I did, indeed, learn something from it.
>
> (Currie 1998: 164)

The second thing to say is that we can use our background knowledge to evaluate whether or not a work of art is reliable. Sometimes we can do this in a straightforward sense: in using our background knowledge to judge whether a work of art is fiction or non-fiction. Rembrandt's self-portraits are works of art, but are generally considered to be a reliable source of knowledge about Rembrandt's appearance (Gaut 2003: 441). We can also use our background knowledge to evaluate whether fictions are reliable. It might seem as if this concedes the position to the sceptic. If I need to use my background knowledge to work out whether *War and Peace* is accurate in its claim "In October 1805, Russian troops were occupying the towns and villages of the Archduchy of Austria ...", then *War and Peace* will not be able to teach me that fact; it will already be there in my background knowledge. However, as we have seen above, we are considering things we can learn from works of art that are not simply beliefs. In such cases, we have to use our background knowledge to judge not whether the work is true, but whether it is *trustworthy*. That is, we judge whether we can trust the work in the influence it has on the weighting of our beliefs or the fineness of our moral perceptions, or in the issues it raises about our values.

The sceptic is unlikely to be impressed. If there are problems with respect to the works being true, then surely the same problems will arise about the works being trustworthy. I think we have to concede that there is no short and simple answer to the sceptic. Deciding whether a work is trustworthy is as difficult as deciding whether a person is trustworthy, and the resources for doing so are similar in each case. It is partly a matter of noticing whether, when it deals with things we think we know about, it gets things right. For example, if we think we know about coping with bereavement, then we can notice how a work deals with bereavement and see whether it corresponds to our views on the matter. If it does, that is a mark in its favour and suggests we can trust the work on other matters. Judging whether or not a work is trustworthy is partly a matter of weighing the evidence (how much of what we know about does it get right?) and partly a matter of feeling (does the work strike us as mature, balanced and sensible?). If the work were a person, would we take their advice on important matters?

This also brings out an important element in our interaction with art. Part of the point of art is that we do not bring our standards to it; rather, we either measure up to, or fall short of, *its* standards. Plato stressed that we are constantly led by, rather than in charge of, our emotions, which is dangerous if our emotions are not in good order. Often, for many of us, our emotions are not in good order; as D. H. Lawrence said, "a man who is *emotionally* educated is as rare as a phoenix" (Lawrence 1936: 539, quoted in Tanner 1976: 103–4). To develop the analogy mentioned above, some works of art can act like friends in whose integrity we have absolute faith. Working out which works of art to trust is a little like working out which friends to trust. How do we decide whether someone is (say) sincere in the grief they are expressing? We might start with the way in which they are expressing their grief. Are they using clichés and simply going through the issues they think they should be going through rather than saying precisely what they want to say? Do they appear to be wallowing in their grief rather than it being a proportional response to what has happened? How are we reacting to them: with compassion, or something like irritation (our own feelings can be a sensitive barometer to others' feelings)? We build an impression as to whether a person – or a work – is trustworthy (Budd 1983).

So far in this chapter we have focused on literary texts. This is the focus of the second and third of the accounts of cognitive engagement (those of Nussbaum and Currie). These accounts particularly suit literary texts because they rely on the narrative elements of a work of art. As we have seen, they apply to an extent to paintings with narrative elements. However, there are two considerations that should stop us simply generalizing from the literary case to paintings. First, the narrative element in painting is relatively limited. Compared to most paintings, *Nighthawks* has a relatively high level of narrative; we are being shown a moment in the lives of four people. However, we are not being shown what brought them to the diner and what their plans are for later. It is true that we can imagine, and the painting encourages us to imagine, their lives beyond the moment Hopper gives us. Nonetheless, what we imagine is not part of the painting. It would be wrong to treat a painting merely as one of a series of panels in a comic in which the other panels are absent. We engage with a painting as it stands; attending to the relations between the various elements of the painting (particularly the painted surface and the depicted scene). The second consideration that should prevent an over-facile generalization from literary works to paintings is that there are many paintings – including all non-figurative paintings – that have no narrative content.

If not through the narrative content, how are we to engage with the cognitive content of a painting? To appreciate what is particularly problematic, we need to return to the account I gave in Chapter 2 of the value of art. Following Budd, I claimed that the value of a work of art as art is the non-instrumental value of the experience we have of the work, provided that experience is had with understanding. In order to bring the problem of the cognitive value of painting into view, we need to say a little more about that experience and in order to do that we need to take a look again at the work of Kant.

For Kant, the principal problem about the judgement that something has aesthetic merit is that it makes a claim to the agreement of other people. To return to the distinction drawn in Chapter 2, when I claim that an object has aesthetic merit, I am claiming something about that object: I am saying that the object is a particular way. This contrasts with the claim that I like the object. In this latter claim, I am not saying that the object is a particular way; I am merely claiming that there is a relation between myself and the object – namely, that I like it. If I claim I like Raoul Dufy's paintings of Nice, I am not claiming that other people should like them as well. I am happy to accept that many people find their brightly coloured optimism jarring. However, if I claim that Dufy's paintings of Nice have aesthetic merit, matters would be different. In this case, were someone to claim that they did *not* have aesthetic merit they would be contradicting me. We cannot both be right; either one or both of us is wrong. As Kant says (using "beautiful" in the sense of "having aesthetic merit"), it would be absurd to say "it is beautiful for me" (Kant 1952: §7).

In Chapter 2, I argued that what enables us to claim the agreement of other people is that our judgement is based on experiencing the work with understanding. We can thus tell a story about, give reasons for, the value of that experience. Our judgement has a claim to the agreement of other people to the extent that they find this story compelling. Kant's account of how an aesthetic judgement can claim agreement from everyone is different. He makes the traditional division of the mind into two: on the one side there are the feelings and sensations, and on the other side are the cognitive elements – beliefs about the way the world is. As we have seen, we do not necessarily agree in judgements grounded in our feelings and sensations; if Dufy's pictures cause me pleasure that is no reason to demand that they cause you pleasure. The same is true of other likes and dislikes. My liking Islay whisky does not lead me to demand that you like Islay whisky (the peaty flavour is not to everyone's taste). On the other hand, if my judgement expresses my beliefs about the way the world is, this will (or should) result in agreement. If I believe the world is a certain way, then, if you do not believe it is that way, one or both of us must be wrong because the world can only ever be one way at any one time. Hence, when it comes to cognitive judgements, the claim to agreement is easy to explain. The judgement claims the world is a certain way, and, if it is that way, then people should agree that it is that way.

We can now see why Kant was troubled by judgements of aesthetic merit making a claim to everyone's agreement. Judgements of aesthetic merit seem to be grounded in the effect that works have on us; that seems to put them on the feelings and sensation side, where agreement cannot be demanded. They do not seem to be grounded on the way the world is – aesthetic merit does not seem part of the world in the way that sticks and stones are – so they do not belong to that side where agreement can be demanded. Hence, Kant's problem: judgements of aesthetic merit make a claim to everyone's agreement, but they seem to stem from that part of the mind that does not necessarily result in everyone's agreement.

Kant's solution is to claim that judgements of aesthetic merit fall between the two parts of the mind so far identified: they are somewhat cognitive, but not too cognitive. That is, he thought they were grounded in the workings of our cognitive machinery, although what is being cranked through the machinery are not beliefs about the way the world is. We can put aside the details of Kant's solution (indeed, my discussion of Kant has been a reconstruction of a line of thought, rather than a proper exposition – in particular, my use of "aesthetic merit" does not correspond exactly to his use of "beauty"). The interesting point for us is the kind of state of mind he thinks goes along with judgements of aesthetic merit. First, they are experiences. Second, they are not simply feelings and sensations; they have a cognitive element. This seems exactly the account we are looking for: looking at works of art requires some cognitive effort, yet it also involves our feelings and sensations.

This account (whether or not it is sufficiently close to the text to attribute it to Kant) raises two difficult problems about whether or not paintings can give us knowledge. The first is about whether paintings can give us knowledge at all, and the second about whether, if they can, that knowledge can be part of the value of art. The first problem arises from the apparent clash between knowledge and experience. The Kantian claim is that cognition is part of the experience of aesthetic merit. For that to be true it would have to be possible for cognitions to feature in our experiences; we would have to be experientially aware of them. It is not obvious, however, that this is possible. Do we *experience* our belief that Paris is the capital of France? Is it something that we feel, as we would feel a headache? Philosophers of mind tell us that we do not experience our cognitive states: that there is "nothing it is like" to have a belief. If that is true, then how can beliefs or knowledge be part of an experience? The second problem concerns value. I argued in Chapter 2 that the value we attribute to art, considered as art, is non-instrumental. The value of our cognitions, however, is instrumental. Knowing that Paris is the capital of France is not good in itself. It is, rather, an instrumental good, enabling me, for example, to board the train for Paris when I would like to get to the capital of France. We are considering whether paintings have a cognitive value. The problem here is that, if there is a cognitive value to paintings, it is of the wrong sort. It would be an instrumental value, while the value we are trying to illuminate is a non-instrumental value. Hence, even if paintings do have a cognitive value, that is not part of the value of paintings when considered as paintings.

Let us, then, return to our example. Above, I claimed that, *prima facie*, *Nighthawks* can give us knowledge, whether it is that cities alienate people from each other, or that bars (coffee or otherwise) are refuges from the dark world outside, or something in the area of the existential loneliness characteristic of modern living. We have left ourselves four problems to solve: whether such knowledge is trivial; whether it is reliable; whether it is part of our experience of the work; and whether it is part of the value of the work.

We already have the elements to solve this problem; we simply need to show how they can be arranged in the right order. We need to show that the cognitive content of the work shows up in the non-instrumentally valuable experience of the work (had with understanding). This will solve the first problem because – as Nussbaum showed – the value would lie in our particular experience of the work rather than the belief abstracted from such an experience. It will also solve the third and fourth problem. Finally, as we have seen, there is no general answer to the second problem; we simply have to use our fallible methods for judging whether the work is trustworthy.

How, then, can we show that the cognitive content of the work shows up in the non-instrumentally valuable experience of the work? In the discussion of forgeries in Chapter 4, I quoted Wollheim's view that discovering something is a forgery does not "raise or lower" the quality of our judgement, but "knocks it sideways". This is because, as I said then, painting is more than simply putting pigment on canvas; it is doing it with a certain aim, governed by a certain set of motivations. Furthermore, when we look at the painting we see it as being governed by these motivations. Our experience of a painting is a matter of engaging with the creative process that led the painter to making the painting the way he or she did. Paintings have an indefinite number of features that we could attend to in engaging with these motivations, including the choice of content, the pictorial organization, the creation of depth and the relation between foreground and background. However, there is also the matter of what the painter puts of himself or herself in the work. It is an old adage that all paintings have elements of self-portrait in them. The painter is externalizing his or her mental states, moving the paint around the canvas until it looks right and captures what the painter hopes to express. This can be an agonizingly slow process; as I remarked above, those unfamiliar with painting are sometimes surprised to hear that a painting can take months, years or even decades to complete. It is this that is part of the value of painting: it puts us in touch with another mind – a mind, furthermore, that has struggled to say something worth saying in as clear a way as they are able. However – to get to the point – this can be done well or badly. Not everyone is capable of putting themselves down honestly on canvas; the temptations of evasion and self-deception are always pressing. Wollheim puts the point as follows:

> Now, it is no small mark of the austerity, of the high seriousness, of art that, while there are several ways in which the activity of making the work can detract from its significance, there is only one way in which it can add to it. It can add to it only when that activity constitutes a process of self-knowledge – with all that that implies: for self-knowledge invariably brings in train self-change, self-reparation. And the creative activity can become a process of self-knowledge when the work of art reflects with sufficient precision some complex constellation of inner states which the artist seeks to externalize. In such cases the artist's activity assumes the character of a benign odyssey, and from which the work of art in turn draws benefit.
>
> Contrast this with ways in which the significance of the work is diminished by the nature of the artist's activity. I shall indicate two ways in which this may come about. First of all, the work of art may insufficiently, too imprecisely, fit the internal states that it is supposed to reflect, and, if this happens, not just any old how, but along a particular dimension, in that something felt to be shameful or degrading or frightening, something … whose outward manifestation could not be steadily contemplated, fails to get externalized, then the artist, in making the work of art, not only fails to acquire self-knowledge, he strenuously attains to self-error …
>
> The second way in which the creative process can contribute negatively to the expressive value of the work is this: The fit between outer and inner need leave nothing to be desired (though it probably will). Nevertheless, the increment in self-knowledge that might reasonably be expected of the creative process does not occur, and the reason

why is to do with the spirit in which the process was undertaken. The work may now bear upon its surface whole truths, not half-truths, but just the motive with which the artist inscribed them upon the surface interferes to prevent his reading them.   (Wollheim 1994a: 11–12)

Wollheim clearly thinks this is the key to the value of paintings: "there is only one way" in which making a work can add to its significance – when the process of self-knowledge that occurs when someone paints avoids the errors he mentions. The solution (or at least part of the solution) to the Kantian problem is this; our experience of the painting has a heavily cognitive character because engaging with the painting just is engaging with the details of the painter's motivations, as we work out what has been placed where on the canvas and why. The question of whether it has been done well or badly takes us back to our problem of judging the work to be trustworthy. We have seen that there is no general answer to that question; we have to make a judgement on the painter's motivations as we engage with them in a way analogous to making a judgement on any human being's motivations in analogous circumstances.

I shall finish this chapter by returning to *Nighthawks*. When we engage with Hopper's motivations in producing this work, what do we find? I have claimed that, *prima facie*, the painting conveys, or reinforces, views about the existential loneliness of modern living. Should such a view be taken seriously? That is, is the painting trustworthy? I shall hesitantly suggest that it is not: that the painting is, rather, sentimental. To substantiate this suggestion it would be as well to be able to say what sentimentality is, something that has proved difficult for philosophers to establish. Anthony Savile has, I think, provided the most illuminating description in his remark that "a sentimental mode of thought is typically one that idealizes its object under the guidance of a desire for gratification and reassurance" (Savile 1982: 241). Why should this be true of *Nighthawks*?

There is a certain kind of character present in contemporary thought. This is a person (usually a man) freed from social bonds, independent, self-reliant and driven by an individual ideal. He is, as Iris Murdoch says, "the hero of almost every contemporary novel" (1985: 7). We might think of examples such as Chandler's Philip Marlowe, or Rick Blaine in *Casablanca*. Such a character seems to fit well with Savile's description. It is very difficult to live such a life well. Even those who have made an heroic effort at it – Jack Kerouac, for example – seem to have been miserable and felt worthless much of the time. It is, however, a very beguiling ideal and playing at living that life, or thinking about living that life, brings a great deal of gratification and reassurance. It promises freedom from the trappings of socialization: the freedom to do what one wants. However, as is characteristic of sentimental thought, it is something that cannot be thought all the way through without reality intruding and spoiling it. Sitting alone late at night in a coffee bar is an activity that has its limits.

I do not mean, in this brief foray into art criticism, to make a major contribution to Hopper studies. Rather, it is supposed to illustrate the Platonic sceptic's point: the seductive power of art is not paired to a necessary link with truth. A picture (or literary text) can be beguiling and misleading. Art can be a source of knowledge, but needs to be treated with some caution. In this respect, as in many other respects, our relations with art are analogous to our relations with people.

8. ART AND MORALITY

Balthus's *Thérèse Dreaming*

The question of whether art can be a source of knowledge touches on the question I shall consider in this chapter: what, if anything, is the connection between art and morality? To talk of *the* connection is misleading because there are many connections between art and morality. I shall briefly discuss two of these first, if only to put them to one side so as to focus on the issues I take to be the most important.

First, there is what we can call "the materials question": the question of the moral appropriateness of the materials from which art is made. One might think that there are some materials – human remains being a paradigm case – where the only appropriate way to treat them is to give them an appropriate interment. We do, or we should, treat human remains with respect. Hence, it might be thought inappropriate to use human remains as the material for a work of art. Certainly, when people have done so, it has caused a furore. In 1984 the Canadian sculptor Rick Gibson rehydrated two human foetuses, freeze-dried them, and exhibited them in the form of earrings (for this he was convicted of outraging public decency). The use of human remains is not unprecedented. One of the Pre-Raphaelites' favourite pigments was "mummy brown"; so called because it was made from ground-up Egyptian mummy. On discovering this, Edward Burne-Jones apparently rushed outside with his tube of paint and buried it in the garden.

What to say about such cases is complicated by our varying attitudes to human remains. It is certainly the case that human remains are exhibited; we have been looking at Bronze Age skeletons and Polynesian shrunken heads for centuries. More recently, Gunther von Hagens has exhibited the Body Worlds exhibition of plasticized corpses. Let us assume that such cases of exhibiting human remains are morally unproblematic (although there is considerable controversy over the moral rectitude of von Hagens's exhibitions). There is still a relevant difference between such cases and those of the arts mentioned above. In the "scientific" case, we are being asked to look at human remains as human remains, and we can take the appropriate attitude when we do so. In the case of art, we are being asked to look at them as works of art and the question is whether doing so is compatible with showing them the appropriate respect. I shall not go into this in part because what it is appropriate to think depends less on art than it does on the broader moral commitments we might have as to what it is or is not appropriate to do with human remains.

It is not only the use of human remains that provokes controversy. There are also works where it is thought that the material used is an unsuitable match to what is depicted. Chris Ofili used elephant dung (a material he often uses in his painting) in a depiction of the Virgin Mary and also as supports for the painting. It was either the use of dung or the representations of female genitalia that are scattered over the painting that vexed the then Mayor of New York, Rudy Giuliani. This is as nothing, however, to the continuing row over Andres Serrano's work *Piss Christ* (1987). This is a polychrome photograph of a crucifix immersed in a jar of urine. The photograph itself does not show the jar; the image, instead, is of the crucifix, backlit, bathed in an orange liquid. Indeed, considered merely as an image, it is rather beautiful. In both these cases there is an apparent conflict between what is depicted (a sacred symbol) and the medium (dung and urine). I say an "apparent" conflict because, before we are able to comment on the works, we need to understand them. One understanding – which grounds the outrage felt towards the work – is that the works are blasphemous. Dung and urine are profane and vulgar, and their use in a depiction of a sacred symbol can only be a calculated insult. An alternative understanding is that it is just this juxtaposition of the sacred and the profane that gives these works their meaning. What the juxtaposition does is drag back or reinvigorate our sense of the sacred as being present in every part of our lives. Deciding which interpretation is appropriate is a matter for critics rather than philosophers. I have discussed these cases to show that there are indeed moral questions that arise out of the use of materials. Understanding what materials are used and why is part of understanding a work, and certain materials are bound to raise moral issues concerning the work.

The second question, which we can label "the notoriety question", concerns whether there are some issues that are morally too sensitive to be part of the subject matter of art. In 1997, the British painter Marcus Harvey exhibited *Myra* in the *Sensation* exhibition at the Royal Academy in London. *Myra* is a large painting (2.7 m × 3.4 m), which consists of the image of the police photograph of Myra Hindley reproduced by means of hundreds of prints of a child's hands. Myra Hindley was one of two people convicted of the abduction, torture and murder of five children. Until her death in prison in 2002, she occupied a peculiar place in British national consciousness as a symbol of evil and an object of considerable hatred. The photograph, which shows a rather hard-faced young woman with a mass of peroxide-blonde hair, is the canonical image of Hindley. The painting caused considerable outrage. There were a number of resignations from the Royal Academy in protest, and, for much of the exhibition, the painting was exhibited behind a Perspex screen to prevent it from being defaced (it was attacked twice before the screen was erected).

The visceral upset that the painting caused to those involved with Hindley's crimes is easy to understand. However, it is not immediately clear what the reasoned objection to the painting could be. It cannot be that art generally ought not to deal with difficult or troubling issues. Perhaps the issue was a sense that the artist was trading on the notoriety of the image for purposes of self-publicity. If this were the case, then the question was not whether works should take difficult or troubling issues as their content, but whether works treat that content seriously. We need to question whether the artist was simply using the content instrumentally (for self-publicity) or whether the work contributed something of value. In short, the issue is one of the quality of the work. On this, commentators were divided. Some thought the work was simply a vehicle for publicity (and hence immoral) while others thought it was a sober and serious meditation on the place of the image of Hindley in British national consciousness. Which of the two views is correct is, again, something we would have to leave to critics rather than philosophers to sort out.

The example of *Myra* is unusual in that it did not depict any obscene or otherwise immoral state of affairs, but rather drew on an image that was morally charged for other reasons. The more usual case is of a work of art that depicts a state of affairs that people find morally problematic. This is certainly the case with the example I shall be discussing in this chapter, Balthus's *Thérèse Dreaming* (1938,). This curious picture measures 150 cm × 130 cm. It depicts a young girl, around twelve years old, sitting in a chair in a room. The picture is painted in a restricted range of rich, warm tones. The figure of the girl is balanced by some furniture and cloth on the left; each object beautifully placed and painted. In the foreground bottom right, a cat laps from a saucer of milk or cream. The most salient feature of the painting is that the girl's left leg is raised so that your gaze is directed between her legs at her white knickers that cover her genitals.

Balthus – or, as he styled himself, Count Klossowski de Rola – was one of the odder painters of the twentieth century. Born in 1908, he largely eschewed modernism, taking instead his characteristic palette and style from Renaissance painters, specifically Piero della Francesca. There is no denying he could paint; many think him one of the most able painters of his time. His *oeuvre* contains paintings that, to me, are difficult to understand. It is not only his pictures of sexualized women and girls (although there are plenty of those); even his other paintings, such as *The Street* (1933), are quite bizarre. After a career laden with honours, he died in 2001.

Thérèse Dreaming is, especially to contemporary sensibilities, shocking. The young girl is prepubescent; she is only just developing breasts. Furthermore, she seems sublimely disinterested; her face is inscrutable, turned away from the viewer. However, in the words of Balthus's biographer, "because of the girl's age, her clothing, and her apparent indifference to the effect of her fierce sexuality, the image is more laden with libido than Titian's Venuses, Goya's Mayas, or Ingres' bordello scenes. Therese emanates eroticism while looking blithely unaware of the fact" (Fox-Webber 1999: 389–90). The cat in the foreground adds to the effect. Cats are often symbols for the erotic but, even if we put that to one side, it is difficult not to see the sensuous licking of the cream as a metaphor for cunnilingus. Finally, we need to remember the title: *Thérèse Dreaming*. Her flared nostrils invite reflection on what it is she is dreaming about. Balthus himself was dismissive of those who found sexuality in his paintings, claiming that any problem was in the mind of the beholder: "Everyone is excited because you can see the little girl's underpants" (*ibid.*: 394).

This picture raises a number of issues. The first is whether it belongs in a book discussing art at all, or whether it is simply pornography. In order to answer this question, we need to have some idea of what it is to be pornographic. In order to decide this, let us put to one side the question of whether or not obscene images are immoral *per se*. That is, I shall (for the moment at least) take no position on the moral status of erotic art and pornography. Instead, I shall investigate the nature (or existence) of the distinction between erotic art and pornography. That is, is there a distinction between erotic images that are art and erotic images that are pornography? If so, what is the nature of this difference?

To remind ourselves of what it is to engage with art as art we need to recall what I said in Chapter 2. I argued for Budd's view that the value of a painting as a painting is the non-instrumental value of the experience of the painting, provided that experience is had with understanding. I further argued that the grounds of the value of the experience can be many and varied. One reason for valuing a painting might be the bold statement it makes about a way of life, or the vision it presents about love and desire. In addition, we might value facets of the organization of the painting, thoughts about how the different features of the painting relate, and how the painting manifests its content: that is, thoughts about how the content of the painting emerges from the colour and spatial relations of the painted surface. Furthermore, it is characteristic of art to reflect on its own content. We are invited not simply to perceive what is given to us, but to think about why it is given to us. What, in presenting us with whatever it is that it presents to us, is a work trying to say? Engaging with an image might provoke our thoughts, and also bring about an affective reaction such as pleasure, wistfulness or awe.

Erotic works will tend to provoke sexual thoughts and feelings in the course of our engagement with them. This certainly seems true of *Thérèse Dreaming* even if those thoughts are only about whether our feelings are appropriate (although, of course, those thoughts might be about other things as well). The question is whether the fact that a work provokes sexual thoughts and feelings takes us into the realm of the pornographic. The terms "erotic art" and "pornography" do not have precise definitions so we will need to do some linguistic tidying up before we can answer this question. I shall follow Levinson and hold that if the purpose of our engagement with a work is to open the way to sexual release (orgasm), we are engaging with the work as pornography (Levinson 2006c). Hence, in the way I am using the words, we *engage* with images more or less pornographically. However, we need not be too purist about which words we apply to our engagement and which words we apply to the works themselves. We can call images for which the appropriate mode of engagement is pornographic, "pornographic images".

Some images are such that the provocation of sexual thoughts and feelings dominates our engagement with them. However, that does not yet mean that we are engaging with them as pornography. Sexual thoughts and feelings are part of human life and as such a legitimate subject matter for artistic exploration. However, if we are engaging with a work as pornography, it is difficult to see how we could at the same time be engaging with it as art. That is, using something as a means to orgasm will detract us from engaging with such matters as the view being put forward, the relation between form and content, and the reflective elements of the work. When we are engaging with something as pornography, we are typically not interested in how and why

141

the content is presented to us as it has been presented to us, but simply in the content. This is why photography is the natural medium for pornography; we do not engage with the various properties of the surface of the photograph, but simply see through the photograph to what it is a photograph of. It is possible for us to engage with a work on one occasion as art, and on another occasion as pornography; what is difficult is doing both at once. On such criteria, I do not think *Thérèse Dreaming* is pornographic (although it would be possible to engage with the image pornographically). The artistic properties are so obvious, the work so accomplished and intriguing, that the appropriate way to engage with it is as art.

Having made the distinction between art and pornography, let us return to our question of the relations between art and morality. What would it be for a work of art to be immoral? We might think that merely representing erotic images would be enough. Clearly, however, more work would need to be done. We would not want to condemn, at a stroke, the long tradition of painting the female nude, although, as I shall discuss in moment, perhaps we ought not to be as sanguine about that tradition as sometimes we are. We could try to be more specific; perhaps nudes are all right provided they are not too graphic. Languid goddesses in a classical setting pass the test but peeking up the skirts of schoolgirls does not. This will not do either for at least two reasons. First, the distinction we are trying to draw here is unclear. Why should the fact that the nude is in a classical setting make a difference? Second, there are plenty of depictions of naked women out of classical settings – even graphic depictions – that appear to be good paintings. Eric Fischl's painting *Bad Boy* (1981) depicts a naked woman lying on a bed, her vagina clearly exposed. A young boy looks on, rifling through her bag behind his back. Strips of harsh sunlight play on the bed, having filtered through the cheap blind. The painting vividly captures a kind of sweaty, value-free world, not particularly to condemn it or laugh at it, but to put it down in front of us.

The way seems open to us to hold that the erotic content of a painting does not in itself determine whether it is moral or immoral; there are erotic paintings that are morally doubtful and erotic paintings that are not morally doubtful (although I still have to say something about how exactly this distinction is made). Although this is a position I would defend, there is a residual puzzle that is worth a small digression to say something about: what we should think of what I called above the "long tradition of painting the female nude". Why do we have such a tradition? Is it as morally neutral as the position stated above would seem to imply?

142

There is one explanation of why we have a tradition of painting the female nude that implies that it is not morally neutral. The answer is (roughly) that men like looking at naked women. This thought surfaces every now and then. Early in the twentieth century, the *Boys' Own Paper* advised its readers to avoid being tempted into masturbation by avoiding art galleries. Norman Tebbit, when a Cabinet Minister, defended newspaper photographs of topless teenagers by arguing that they provide the working-class equivalent of the middle- and upper-class experience of art. To reply that there is a categorical difference, that engagement with newspaper photographs is pornographic while engagement with paintings is artistic, does not quite settle the issue. The question remains: why is there a long tradition of engaging artistically with pictures of naked women rather than (for instance) of cats and dogs?

The position should not be overstated. The tradition of the nude includes depictions of both women and men (especially if one counts depictions of Christ on the cross). Even if we grant this, as has been pointed out by Kenneth Clark in his classic study *The Nude*, while the male nude was dominant until the late fifteenth century, the female nude has dominated since (Clark 1960: 343). Views on the explanation for this dominance differ depending on one's intellectual presuppositions. The explanation need not be simple, of course; there might be a variety of factors that kept men behind the easel and women in front of it. However, it is likely that prominent among these reasons will be the general political and societal factors that explain why there have historically been fewer women doctors, lawyers and prime ministers. The way society was structured meant that being an artist was a career open only (or mainly) to men, who had a supply of women available to model for them. Once it had become established that "the nude" (i.e. "the female nude") was a canonical subject for depiction, it became – in itself – a way of capturing, and expressing, certain formal achievements. Clark neatly captures the way in which the female nude grew to be formally satisfactory:

[I]t is arguable that the female body is plastically more rewarding on what, at their first submission, seem to be purely abstract grounds. Since Michelangelo few artists have shared a Florentine passion for shoulders, knees, and other small knobs of form. They have found it easier to compose harmoniously the larger unit of a woman's torso; they have been grateful for its smoother transitions, and above all they have discovered analogies with satisfying geometrical forms, the oval, the ellipsoid and the sphere. But may not this argument reverse the order of cause and effect? Is there, after all, any reason

> why certain quasi-geometrical shapes should be satisfying except
> that they are simplified statements of the forms which please us in a
> woman's body? (Clark 1960: 344)

If we assume something like this is correct, it leaves us with a problem. If doubtful social structures have given us a "way of seeing" (to use the title of an influential book on this very point; Berger 1972), then what is the moral status of the female nude? The problem is not that a certain artistic practice was born of injustice; the simple fact that something had its origins in injustice does not entail that it cannot be appreciated independently of that injustice. Kant rightly repudiates the Rousseauean for harping on "the vanity of the great who spend the sweat of the people on such superfluous things" while we are trying to enjoy the Taj Mahal (Kant 1952: §2). Rather, the problem is that the tradition of the female nude continues to reinforce such injustice; it gives us a "way of seeing" that places women in one position and men in another.

It is difficult to know what to do with this conclusion. Because the female nude has been such a dominant tradition, it is the tradition in which some great artists have done some great work that it would seem absurd to ignore (in addition, ignoring them would not remove whatever pernicious social effects they are said to have). In addition, while not disputing the facts of the case, one might be wary of allowing moral considerations free reign in the realm of relations between the sexes; the erotic is probably not a realm that can bear too much moral transparency. Whatever one's views on these two responses, it is also open to female artists to "recapture" the nude and make it rather less a one-sided affair (Nead 1992: 34–83). As society becomes less patriarchal, traditions in painting might become more balanced. I am not sure there is much left to say on the issue apart from the rather banal injunction that, in engaging with the value of paintings in the tradition of the female nude, one should bear in mind that the tradition emerged from, and embodies, unjust social practices.

My answer to the question of why there was a long tradition of the female nude is deflationary in comparison to some others. In Chapter 2, I considered the semiotic view: the idea that paintings are signs in a symbol system and T. J. Clark's claim that the nakedness of *Olympia* is a sign of class. As I argued there, the flexibility introduced by the semiotic view allows that signs can have meanings that are not tied in any simple way to the constraints of what can be seen. Thus, the nude can be interpreted in ways that seem to go beyond the scope of vision; Lynda Nead goes as far as to claim that it "strains the value oppositions of Western metaphysics to their limits" (1992: 25). Indeed, this area provides a stark illustration of those whose interpretations of paintings are constrained by what can be seen, and those who can work with the looser "associations" of semiotics (as can be seen in *ibid.*: 5-33).

So far, in the discussion of whether the content of a work can be immoral, I have considered the difference between regarding a work pornographically and regarding it as art and concluded (following Levinson) that it is difficult if not impossible to do both at the same time. I then asked what it was that made a work immoral; it was not simply being a picture with an erotic content because there would appear to be works with immoral content that are not immoral (the example I gave was Fischl's *Bad Boy*). I then digressed with a discussion of whether the long tradition of the female nude itself raised moral issues. Having had that discussion, we can return to our main theme. If it is not by depicting the immoral states of affairs, how then can a work be immoral? To answer this we need to return to the thought that art reflects on its own content. It not only shows us something but, by the way in which it shows us, says something about what is shown. Fischl's picture does not show the actions of either the woman or the boy in a positive light. If it did, that is, if it somehow celebrated or sanctioned their behaviour, it would be more problematic. If a work portrays a morally problematic state of affairs and then manifests an immoral attitude to it (as Hume says, the content is portrayed "without being marked with the proper characters of blame and disapprobation"; Hume [1757] 1993b: 152) then the work is immoral.

Rather than returning to a direct discussion of our example, I shall consider a different example from which I hope we can draw lessons to apply to Balthus's problematic picture. Clear examples of immoral works are few and far between. Pornographic images that celebrate the humiliation of their subjects or images that display certain racial groups as subhuman could provide examples. My example comes from film: the portrayal, in D. W. Griffiths's *The Birth of a Nation*, of the Ku Klux Klan heroically restoring order to the Southern States of America after the Civil War. This film portrays evil events in a positive light; having demonized the black characters, one such (Gus) is tried in a kangaroo court and killed by the Klan. What is the relation between these features of the film and the value of the film as a work of art?

One option would be to claim that there are two different judgements to be made: an aesthetic judgement and a moral judgement. The first judgement is whether or not *The Birth of a Nation* works as a film. The second judgement is whether or not *The Birth of a Nation* is or is not immoral. In judging the first, we would focus on such things as whether it was well shot, well paced and compelling, the quality of the camerawork and editing, and the overall look of the film. In judging the second, we would simply adjudicate as to whether the attitude it took is moral or immoral. Support for this option can be found in ordinary language. We sometimes use the word "aesthetic" to refer to how things look or sound. For example, we might say that while a bridge is a success from an economic point of view it is a disaster from an aesthetic point of view. What we would seem to be saying here is something as simple as that it does not look nice. Thus, we could say that *The Birth of a Nation*, while a disaster from a moral point of view, is a success from an aesthetic point of view.

The hard distinction between aesthetic and moral value is, as I have said, reflected in some aspects of our ordinary language. To that extent, keeping the aesthetic and moral judgements distinct is a viable option. However, it is difficult to keep the judgements distinct once we engage with the work of art as a work of art. To engage with the film as a series of images that are more or less well constructed is to fail to engage with it with understanding. It misses out a whole raft of features of the film: namely, the way it presents the events that unfolded at a certain time and place in the world.

One can accept that in engaging with a work of art one has to engage not only with the way it looks but also with its content, but still insist on a distinction between aesthetic (or artistic) judgements and moral judgements. Art is different from life. That there are no unicorns does not prevent me from producing paintings of unicorns. In general, the realm of art releases us from the constraints imposed by dull reality. In fiction, we can travel faster than the speed of light, ride broomsticks, rule kingdoms and even make two plus two equal five. That is, the claims made within art do not have to track what is true in the actual world. It might be that the Ku Klux Klan is an immoral organization in the actual world but we are not concerned with the actual world. *The Birth of a Nation* is not history, but fiction. There is no need to pass judgement on what is true or false, moral or immoral, when we are thinking about the content of a fiction.

Once again, there is something to be said for this view. None of us (I take it) think that it is all right to nail kittens to planks of wood or set fire to them, yet it would be precious to think that Tom and Jerry cartoons should be condemned for condoning just such actions (although the Itchy and Scratchy cartoons in *The Simpsons* might prompt us to re-evaluate this judgement; what exactly have we been laughing at all these years?). The violence takes place in a cartoon, and the content of a cartoon is immune to judgements that we would make were it to take place in the actual world. Such cartoons do not aspire to be taken seriously. However, as we saw in the previous chapter, some works of art do aspire to be taken seriously and convey a view about the workings of the actual world. *The Birth of a Nation* is a vehicle for a number of propositions, one of which is that people need to come together to sort things out in times of crisis. Some aspects of that claim are clearly sensible. Other aspects, such as those exemplified by the actions of the Ku Klux Klan, are not so. In short, the content of some works of art fall within the domain of morality and can be evaluated in those terms. This is not to say that there is nothing to be said for *The Birth of a Nation*; there is plenty to be said for it. However, among those things that can be said about it *as a film* is that its content is not all we could wish it to be.

How does *Thérèse Dreaming* fit in with these points? We could attempt to separate the aesthetic aspects of the painting from its morally problematic aspects. That is, we could try, when looking at it as a painting, to see it in purely painterly terms, ignoring its depictive content. This was the course of action recommended by Clive Bell in his book *Art* (cited in the Introduction): "To appreciate art we need to bring with us nothing but a sense of form and colour and a knowledge of three-dimensional space" (Bell 1928: 27). Thus instead of seeing Thérèse in her recumbent posture, we would see a selection of solids in pictorial space, standing in harmonious colour and spatial relations to each other. However, there are two problems that undermine the view that this is the right way to see the picture. First, it is unmotivated. An understanding of the picture involves an understanding of its figurative content. It would require a powerful argument to convince us that we should ignore the figurative content, and there is no such argument. Second, it is psychologically very difficult to look at the picture in the way Bell suggests; we simply cannot help seeing it as a girl sitting on a chair.

What of the claim that we should see *Thérèse Dreaming* merely as a fiction, and excuse it from the moral claims that obtain in the real world? We cannot simply generalize from *The Birth of a Nation* to *Thérèse Dreaming*; there are some interesting differences. When we watch the film, we watch events as they unfold without our involvement. It is not us who is threatening Flora or hunting down Gus. All we are called on to do, if anything, is pass judgement on what is depicted for us. However, in *Thérèse Dreaming*, we are being invited to see the world from the point of view Balthus gives us: we are invited to look up the skirt of a prepubescent girl and, what is more, there is nothing in the picture to indicate that we should feel uncomfortable doing so. Indeed, as discussed, there are various features of the painting that encourage us to take a sexualized attitude to it. In short, the picture invites us to be complicit in taking sexual pleasure in looking up the skirt of a pre-pubescent girl.

It looks, then, as if the option of simply saying that *Thérèse Dreaming* is a fiction and thus not subject to real-world morality is not available to us. What is morally problematic about the picture is that engaging with it means *our* taking on a perspective that we do not want to take on. We do not have the option of regarding the picture as depicting a fictional world that might have a moral code different from that of the actual world. The picture asks moral questions of us, and we are rooted in the actual world. Someone who favoured the view that we should not apply actual world moral norms to fic-tion might question this. Instead of regarding Thérèse as being in a fictional world and us as being in an actual world, why not regard the whole state of affairs as fictional? That is, when we engage with fiction we do not engage as our actual selves rooted in the actual world but as our fictional selves as part of Thérèse's world. Because we are fictional selves rather than actual selves, there is no reason why we should have to apply actual-world morality; after all, it is only a picture.

In case the issue is not clear, consider an analogy. When you are playing a game of make-believe (say Cowboys and Indians), it is not your actual-world self observing an attack by the Indians. Rather, it is your fictional self (a cowboy) being attacked by Indians. You are able to do things in the game (kill people) that you would not do in the actual world. Similarly, when you regard Thérèse, you might regard yourself as someone in the same fictional world as Thérèse. As with games of make-believe, there is no reason to think that what would apply in the actual world (it being perverse to take sexual pleasure in prepubescents) applies in the fictional world. There is a puzzle here that merits attention (Walton 2006). Although I have no answer to the question of why we cannot suspend our actual-world moral sensibilities, I nevertheless think that we cannot; it is our actual-world identities that are in play when we look at the picture. Why this is I do not know, although my suspicion is that it stems from deep issues in the structure of our engagement with the arts.

What, then, is the final judgement on *Thérèse Dreaming*? As with any work of art, an account of what it would be to fully understand the work will be complicated, dealing with issues of form and content, Balthus's intentions and the circumstances and context of its production. However, within that account will be some acknowledgement that the picture invites us to take a view (both literally and metaphorically) that is morally problematic and that this is a flaw in the work: not only a moral flaw, but a flaw in engaging with the work as art. *Thérèse Dreaming* is not only an unusual work, but also strays into the territory of paedophilia, the secular world's touchstone of the morally problematic.

Our example in this chapter has been a work that represents a state of affairs one might find in the world. We have focused on the question of whether that situation and the way it is presented are morally dubious and, if so, what difference that makes to the value of the painting considered as a painting. This focus might suggest that the question of art and morality arises only with works of art that represent states of affairs. This might seem a happy result because it is not obvious what moral issue could arise from (for example) instrumental music or non-figurative painting. How could a succession of notes or a melange of colours be moral or immoral? To see how a non-figurative work could have moral content, recall the example I considered in Chapter 2: Rothko's murals for the Four Seasons Restaurant in New York. I reported Rothko as saying that he hoped "to ruin the appetite of every son of a bitch who ever eats in that room". This, together with other remarks he made, suggests that he thought that members of the wealthy elite who understood his paintings would, in virtue of doing so, feel indicted. Newman went further, claiming (rather hubristically) that "if my work were properly understood, it would be the end of state capitalism and totalitarianism" (1993: 766). There are musical works that can also serve as examples. It is difficult to listen to Beethoven's symphonies (the Third, the Fifth and the Ninth in particular) without understanding them as embodying a highly moralized view of life. Indeed, having originally dedicated the Third to Napoleon, Beethoven ripped the dedication page away on learning that Napoleon had declared himself Emperor. This suggests that Beethoven thought there was something about the symphony that took a stand on matters such as freedom from tyranny and the established order.

We saw, in Chapter 6, Adorno's argument that responding to the horrors of the modern world required more than producing works with horrific content. An adequate response also required changes in the form of the work. We can start to make sense of how artistic form can have morally evaluable content by looking at a splendidly vitriolic exchange between two aestheticians from early in the last century: Ernst Bloch and Georg Lukács. Both men were committed Marxists and both endorsed "the reflection thesis". This thesis can be found in the following passage from Marx:

> In the social production of their existence, men inevitably enter into
> definite relations, which are independent of their will, namely rela-

tions of production appropriate to a given stage in the development of their material forces of production. The totality of these relations of production constitutes the economic structure of society, the real foundation, on which arises a legal and political superstructure and to which correspond definite forms of social consciousness. The mode of production of material life conditions the general process of social, political, and intellectual life. It is not the consciousness of men that determines their existence, but their social existence that determines their consciousness.   (Marx [1859] 1994: 211)

The core thought is that works of art belong in "the superstructure": that is, they are a reflection of the social and economic conditions that prevailed at the time at which they were created. This immediately raises the possibility of moral approbation or condemnation: if they endorse unfair social and economic conditions they are applauded; if they celebrate unfair economic and social conditions they are condemned. The problem, however, is that it is very unclear what art needs to do to manifest the right sort of reflection. Bloch thought the fragmentary nature of expressivist painting should be applauded because it was an accurate reflection of the contradictory nature of capitalism (Bloch [1938] 1980). Lukács, however, thought expressivist painting ought to be condemned as it is an uncritical reflection of the turmoil in the mind of the bourgeois at a critical moment for capitalism (Lukács [1938] 1980). Bloch's view was that, in pedalling classicism, Lukács favoured "culture without temperament" (Bloch [1938] 1980: 25). For Lukács, Bloch sought to "confine [himself] to reproducing whatever manifests itself truly and on the surface" (Lukács [1938] 1980). It is clear that, without some considerable efforts at clarification, the "reflection thesis" will provide no clear grounds for applauding or condemning non-figurative works.

Adorno's work – which is a great deal more sophisticated than that of Bloch or Lukács – follows in this tradition (Adorno 2004). He sees worthwhile works of art as having a dual nature. On the one hand, and this draws on traditional aesthetic thought, they are autonomous objects; they have no practical function. Because they stand aloof from the world they have the potential to provide something independent against which we can measure our lives. On the other hand, as we saw in Chapter 6, they are in perennial danger of contributing to the theodicy: the task of reconciling ourselves to the world. Less worthwhile works of art he sees simply as part of "the culture industry", whose function is that of "bread and circuses": something to distract the civic population from the unjust conditions in which they live.

With this theoretical edifice in place (of which the above is a very simplified description), Adorno is able to indulge in some highly moralized art criticism. Among the worthwhile, Schoenberg's difficult and atonal music manifests a truthful reluctance to evade the difficulties of social existence. In contrast, Stravinsky's neoclassical period (during which his music drew on traditional tonal forms) is an evasion. Unfortunately, Adorno spoils the appearance of objectivity by using his theory as an excuse for some fairly crude lambasting of art that he does not find worthwhile; this is particularly so in his perorations against jazz (Adorno 1941).

The view that all art, not only art that represents states of affairs, can be morally significant does not require that we endorse a Marxist reflection thesis in either its crude or its sophisticated form. Instead, we can take a step back and consider morality in the broadest sense, as attempting to answer the question 'How should one live?' (Williams 1985). Should one devote one's life to the pursuit of money? To alleviate misery? To pleasure? To idleness? The values one pursues are manifest in the choices one makes, and this includes the choice of whether to engage with art, and, if so, the choice of art with which one engages. Here, the enormous variety of the links between art and the emotions becomes evident. Compare, for example, the different moral worlds suggested by Roger Scruton's lament over the decline of the formal dance and Jack Kerouac's fictionalized account of listening to jazz in Chicago:

> It is obvious that dancing has social consequences – particularly on the attitudes through which men and women come together in quest of a partner. Traditional dances had to be learned – often by a long process which began in childhood. (Think of the gavotte, the gig, or the stately saraband.) They were not forms of abandon, but exercises in self-control. They required the dancer to understand steps, patterns, formation, and sequences; they required him to fit his gestures to the movement of his partner and to the pattern of the whole. In formation dancing, you also relinquish your partner to dance with others whom you may not know. In this way the sexual motive is moderated by its very invocation.   (Scruton 1997: 498)

> Something would come of it yet. There's always more, a little further – it never ends. They sought to find new phrases after Shearing's explorations; they tried hard. They writhed and twisted and blew. Every now and then a clear harmonic cry gave new suggestions of

a tune that would someday be the only tune in the world and raise men's souls to joy. They found it, they lost, they wrestled for it, they found it again, they laughed, they moaned – and Dean sweated at the table and told them to go, go, go. At nine o'clock in the morning everybody – musicians, girls in slacks, bartenders, and the one little skinny, unhappy trombonist – staggered out of the club into the great roar of the Chicago day to sleep until the wild bop night again.

(Kerouac 1972: 227–8)

Regardless of whether you think Scruton is right in thinking that the kind of life exemplified by court dances has the moral edge over the kind of life exemplified by bebop jazz, there is something to the thought that the art with which we choose to engage and the way in which we choose to engage with it manifests our values. This is, I think, the kindest way to interpret Newman's claim above that his paintings, properly understood, would "be the end of state capitalism and totalitarianism". The paintings Newman had in mind are non-figurative: characteristically, a slab of colour with a stripe (or "zip") down the side. They are exemplars of something the value of which could only be non-instrumental. Therefore, they stand in stark contrast to the value characteristic of capitalism: exchange value. To understand a Newman painting is to understand that there are things in the world that are valuable only in themselves; they are not valuable because of the things one could get for them. Newman's hope, I take it, is that once someone appreciates the strength of this value, they will look askance on the constant seeking of value in the buying and selling of the capitalist system.

Works of art, even non-figurative works, invite us to endorse, if not a view of life, at least something relevant to the answer to the question of how we ought to live. I suggested, in the previous chapter, that the view of life expressed by *Nighthawks* was sentimental: that the view of life it expressed was something that had not been properly thought through as a life that could be lived. There are examples of works that express a view of life that appears, at least at first sight, as more authentic. In his *David*, Michelangelo was putting forward a view of humans as beings of stature and dignity: perhaps a view in contrast to the excessive self-abasement and humility characteristic of some versions of Christianity. To be clear, I am not claiming that we should judge works of art according to whether they conform to, or go against, our narrow conception of what is good and bad. The claim is rather that works of art sometimes express something more general: something I am rather grandly calling "a view of life". This might express a view within the scope of what we take to be good or bad or it might express – as the Bohemian and Beat works have down the ages – a view of life that downplays the moral in favour of a view of life that foregrounds the beautiful.

Accepting that works of art can manifest a view of life allows us to situate art alongside other matters that engage us. Our view of life can be manifest in other interactions with the world, whether in the way we lay the table for dinner or the way in which we dress. We express ourselves in the way we alter the appearance of our environment and in the kinds of environment in which we feel comfortable. I do not want to downplay the distinction between our general engagement with our visual environment and our engagement with the visual arts (as have some others; Dewey 1934). I have argued (particularly in Chapter 2, but also in Chapter 7) that understanding and appreciating works of art can be a difficult and time-consuming endeavour. However, once we have asked ourselves how we ought to live we should pay some attention, in formulating our answer, not only to matters such as loving our neighbour or eradicating poverty, but also to other aspects of our engagement with the world. We should do this not only because the way things appear might make people happier, or encourage the civic virtues, but because the way things appear is an important matter in itself.

The relation between art and morality is a fitting discussion to end this book for it brings to mind two themes that have been either explicit or implicit in our discussion so far. The first is that engaging with art is not a process that is cut off from life; such engagement involves bringing our knowledge and experience to bear as well as measuring our thoughts and attitudes against what we find in art. The second is that – contrary to assumptions often made in ethical and political philosophy – the values we find in art (whether beauty, or, more broadly, aesthetic merit) deserve consideration in their own right. A satisfactory life is not a life in which we should always strive to do the right thing; we should make room to sometimes do the beautiful thing.

FURTHER READING

Although books like this are helpful, they are no substitute for reading the works of philosophers themselves. I would recommend the papers collected in anthologies such as Peter Lamarque and Stein Haugom Olsen (eds), *Aesthetics and the Philosophy of Art* (2004) and Steven M. Cahn and Aaron Meskin (eds), *Aesthetics: A Comprehensive Anthology* (2007). These contain many of the papers discussed in the text. What follows are suggestions for books on the individual topics. That a book is omitted from this list does not imply I do not think it worth reading; it is rather that the works cited here are those that I think best suited to following up ideas I have introduced.

CHAPTER 1: WHAT IS ART?

The literature on the definition of art is voluminous. Stephen Davies's *Definitions of Art* (1991) is a good guide, and Chapter 6 of Jason Gaiger's *Aesthetics and Painting* (2008) has a good discussion of the relevance of modernism. Dominic Lopes's *Beyond Art* (forthcoming) should give new life to a rather tired debate.

CHAPTER 2: THE VALUE OF ART

Rather surprisingly, there is not as much written on the value of art as one would expect. Malcolm Budd's *Values of Art* (1995) is unsurpassed. The semiotic theory of art gets a more sympathetic hearing in Chapter 4 of Gaiger's *Aesthetics and Painting*.

CHAPTER 3: EXPRESSION

Although there is a great deal written on the expression of emotion in music, there is not much written on the expression of emotion in the visual arts. A good guide to this – and other aspects of paintings – is Dominic Lopes's *Sight and Sensibility* (2005).

CHAPTER 4: FORGERIES, COPIES AND VARIATIONS

There is a useful anthology edited by Denis Dutton on the topic of forgery, although it can be difficult to find: *The Forger's Art* (1983). There are several accounts of van Meegeren's career; the one from which I derived my information was Frank Wynne's *I was Vermeer* (2007).

CHAPTER 5: INTENTION AND INTERPRETATION

The debate on intention has principally occurred in papers, many of which are discussed in the text. A good recent book is Paisley Livingston's *Art and Intention* (2007).

CHAPTER 6: BEAUTY AND UGLINESS

Matthew Kieran's *Revealing Art* (2005) contains a number of interesting discussions, including much on beauty and ugliness.

CHAPTER 7: ART AND KNOWLEDGE

Although about literature rather than about painting, Martha Nussbaum's collection of essays *Love's Knowledge* (1990a) contains much that is interesting on learning from art.

CHAPTER 8: ART AND MORALITY

Once again, this debate is carried our principally through papers. A good, short guide to Adorno's thought can be found in Chapter 6 of Andy Hamilton's *Aesthetics and Music* (2007).

BIBLIOGRAPHY

Adorno, T. 1941. "On Popular Music". *Studies in Philosophy and Social Science* **9**(1): 17–48.

Adorno, T. 2004. *Aesthetic Theory*. London: Continuum.

Adorno, T., W. Benjamin, E. Bloch, B. Brecht & G. Lukacs (eds) 1980. *Aesthetics and Politics*. London: Verso.

Anfam, D. 1990. *Abstract Expressionism*. London: Thames & Hudson.

Bacon, F. [1607] 1931. "*Of Beauty*". In *Philosophies of Beauty from Socrates to Robert Bridges: Being the Sources of Aesthetic Theory*, E. F. Carritt (ed.), 56. Oxford: Clarendon Press.

Beardsley, M. C. 1981. *Aesthetics: Problems in the Philosophy of Criticism*. Indianapolis, IN: Hackett.

Beardsley, M. C. 1982. "Aesthetic Experience". In *The Aesthetic Point of View: Selected Essays*, M. J. Wreen & D. M. Callen (eds), 285–97. Ithaca, NY: Cornell University Press.

Beardsley, M. C. 2004. "An Aesthetic Definition of Art". In *Aesthetics and the Philosophy of Art: The Analytic Tradition*, P. Lamarque & S. H. Olson (eds), 55–62. Oxford: Blackwell. [Originally published in *What is Art?*, H. Curtler (ed.), 15–29 (New York: Haven Publications, 1983).]

Bell, C. 1928. *Art*. London: Chatto & Windus.

Berger, J. 1972. *Ways of Seeing*. Harmondsworth: Penguin.

Bloch, E. 1980. "Discussing Expressionism". See Adorno *et al.* (1980), 16–27. [Originally published in German as "*Diskussionen über Expressionismus*", *Das Wort* 6 (June 1938), 103–112.]

Bourriaud, N. 2002. *Relational Aesthetics*. Dijon: Les Presses du Reel.

Breslin, J. E. B. 1993. *Mark Rothko: A Biography*. Chicago, IL: University of Chicago Press.

Briggs, J. B. 1989. *Joe Bob Briggs Goes to the Drive-In*. Harmondsworth: Penguin.

Budd, M. 1983. "Belief and Sincerity in Poetry". In *Pleasure, Preference and Value*, E. Schaper (ed.), 137–57. Cambridge: Cambridge University Press.

Budd, M. 1985. *Music and the Emotions*. London: Routledge & Kegan Paul.

Budd, M. 1995. *Values of Art: Pictures, Poetry, Music*. Harmondsworth: Penguin.

Budd, M. 2008a. "The Characterization of Aesthetic Qualities by Essential Metaphors and Quasi-Metaphors". In his *Aesthetic Essays*, 142–53. Oxford: Oxford University Press. [Originally published in *British Journal of Aesthetics* (2006) **46**(2): 133–43.]

Budd, M. 2008b. "The Intersubjective Validity of Aesthetic Judgements". In his *Aesthetic*

Essays, 62–104. Oxford: Oxford University Press. [Originally published in *British Journal of Aesthetics* (2007) **47**(4): 333–71.]

Cahn, S. M. & A. Meskin (eds) 2007. *Aesthetics: A Comprehensive Anthology*. Oxford: Blackwell.

Clark, K. 1960. *The Nude*. London: John Murray.

Clark, T. J. 1985. *The Painting of Modern Life: Paris in the Art of Manet and his Followers*. London: Thames & Hudson.

Coxton, A. 2010. *Louise Bourgeois*. London: Tate Publishing.

Currie, G. 1989. *The Ontology of Art*. Basingstoke: Palgrave Macmillan.

Currie, G. 1995. "The Moral Psychology of Fiction". *Australasian Journal of Philosophy* **73**(2): 250–59.

Currie, G. 1998. "Realism of Character and the Value of Fiction". In *Aesthetics and Ethics: Essays at the Intersection*, J. Levinson (ed.), 161–81. Cambridge: Cambridge University Press.

Danto, A. 1986. "The End of Art". In his *The Philosophical Disenfranchisement of Art*, 81–115. New York, NY: Columbia University Press. [Originally published in *The Death of Art*, B. Lang (ed.) (New York: Haven Publications, 1984).]

Danto, A. 1995. "The Artworld". In *The Philosophy of Art: Readings Ancient and Modern*, A. Neill & A. Ridley, 201–12. New York: McGraw-Hill. [Originally published in *Journal of Philosophy* **61**(19), American Philosophical Association Eastern Division Sixty-First Annual Meeting (15 October, 1964), 571–84.]

Davies, S. 1991. *Definitions of Art*. Ithaca, NY: Cornell University Press.

Dewey, J. 1934. *Art as Experience*. New York: Minton, Balch.

Dickie, G. 1974. *Art and Aesthetic*. Ithaca, NY: Cornell University Press.

Dutton, D. 1983. *The Forger's Art: Forgery and the Philosophy of Art*. Berkeley, CA: University of California Press.

Dutton, D. 2002. "Artistic Crimes". In *Arguing About Art: Contemporary Philosophical Debates*, A. Neill & A. Ridley (eds), 100–110. London: Routledge. [Originally published in *British Journal of Aesthetics* **19**(4) (1965): 304–14.]

Dutton, D. 2003. "Authenticity in Art". See Levinson (2003), 258–74.

Elger, D. 2009. *Gerhard Richter: A Life in Painting*. Chicago, IL: University of Chicago Press.

Forceville, C. 2005. "Visual Representations of the Idealized Cognitive Model of Anger in the Asterix Album La Zizanie". *Journal of Pragmatics* **37**(1): 69–88.

Fox-Webber, N. 1999. *Balthus: A Biography*. London: Weidenfeld & Nicholson.

Gaiger, J. 2008. *Aesthetics and Painting*. London: Continuum.

Gaut, B. 2003. "Art and Knowledge". See Levinson (2003), 436–50.

Geuss, R. 1999. "Art and Theodicy". In his *Morality, Culture and History*, 78–115. Cambridge: Cambridge University Press.

Godfrey, T. 1998. *Conceptual Art*. London: Phaidon.

Goldie, P. & E. Schellekens (eds) 2007. *Philosophy and Conceptual Art*. Oxford: Clarendon Press.

Goodman, N. 1976. *The Languages of Art*. Indianapolis, IN: Hackett.

Greenberg, C. 1992. "Modernist Painting". In *Art in Modern Culture: An Anthology of Critical Texts*, F. Frascina & J. Harris (eds), 308–14. London: Phaidon. [Originally published in his *Art and Culture* (Boston, MA: Beacon Press, 1961).]

Hamilton, A. 2007. *Aesthetics and Music*. London: Continuum.

Harrison, C. & P. Wood (eds) 1993. *Art in Theory 1900–1990: An Anthology of Changing Ideas*. Oxford: Blackwell.

Hegel, G. W. F. [1842] 1979. *Introduction to Aesthetics*. Oxford: Clarendon Press.

Hughes, R. 1991. *Nothing If Not Critical: Selected Essays on Art and Artists*. London: Harvill.

Hume, D. 1993a. *Selected Essays*, S. Copley & A. Edgar (eds). Oxford: Oxford University Press.

Hume, D. [1757] 1993b. "Of the Standard of Taste". See Hume (1993a), 133–54.

Hume, D. [1757] 1993c. "Of Tragedy". See Hume (1993a), 126–33.

Hursthouse, R. 1992. "Truth and Representation". In *Philosophical Aesthetics: An Introduction*, O. Hanfling (ed.), 239–96. Oxford: Blackwell.

Kant, I. 1952. *The Critique of Judgement*. Oxford: Oxford University Press.

Kerouac, J. 1972. *On the Road*. Harmondsworth: Penguin.

Kieran, M. 2005. *Revealing Art*. London: Routledge.

Kristeller, P. O. 1951. "The Modern System of the Arts: A Study in the History of Aesthetics (I)". *Journal of the History of Ideas* **12**(4): 496–527.

Kristeller, P. O. 1952. "The Modern System of the Arts: A Study in the History of Aesthetics (II)". *Journal of the History of Ideas* **13**(1): 17–46.

Lamarque, P. & S. H. Olsen (eds) 2004. *Aesthetics and the Philosophy of Art*. Oxford: Blackwell.

Lawrence, D. H. (ed.) 1936. *Phoenix: The Posthumous Papers of D. H. Lawrence*. London: Heinemann.

Lessing, A. 1965. "What is Wrong with a Forgery?" *Journal of Aesthetics and Art Criticism* **23**(4): 461–71.

Levinson, J. 1979. "Defining Art Historically". In his *Music, Art and Metaphysics: Essays in Philosophical Aesthetics*, 3–25. Ithaca, NY: Cornell University Press.

Levinson, J. 1996a. *The Pleasures of Aesthetics*. Ithaca, NY: Cornell University Press.

Levinson, J. 1996b. "Intention and Interpretation in Literature". See Levinson (1996a), 175–213. [This is a revised version of his essay "Intention and Interpretation: A Last Look", in *Intention and Interpretation*, G. Iseminger (ed.) (Philadelphia, PA: Temple University Press, 1992), 221–56.]

Levinson, J. 1996c. "Messages in Art". See Levinson (1996a), 224–41. [Originally published in *Australasian Journal of Philosophy* **73**(2) (1995), 184–98.]

Levinson, J. 1996d. "Work and Oeuvre". See Levinson (1996a), 242–73.

Levinson, J. (ed.) 2003. *The Oxford Handbook of Aesthetics*. Oxford: Oxford University Press.

Levinson, J. 2006a. *Contemplating Art: Essays in Aesthetics*. Oxford: Clarendon Press.

Levinson, J. 2006b. "Hypothetical Intentionalism: Statement, Objections, and Replies". See Levinson (2006a), 302–11. [Originally published in *Is There a Single Right Interpretation?*, M. Krausz (ed.), 309–18 (University Park, PA: University of Pennsylvania Press, 2002).]

Levinson, J. 2006c. "Erotic Art and Pornographic Pictures". In his *Contemplating Art: Essays in Aesthetics*, 259–71. Oxford: Clarendon Press. [Originally published in *Philosophy and Literature* **29**(1) (2005), 228–40.]

Lewis, M. 1960. "The Monotone Symphony, March 9, 1960". www.artep.net/kam/symphony.html (accessed August 2012).

LeWitt, S. 1993. "Paragraphs on Conceptual Art". See Harrison & Wood (1993), 834–7. [Originally published in *Artforum* **5**(10) (June 1967), 79–83.]

Livingston, P. 2007. *Art and Intention: A Philosophical Study*. Oxford: Oxford University Press.

Lopes, D. M. 2005. *Sight and Sensibility: Evaluating Pictures*. Oxford: Oxford University Press.

Lopes, D. M. 2008. "Nobody Needs a Theory of Art". *Journal of Philosophy* **105**(3): 109–27.

Lopes, D. forthcoming. *Beyond Art*. Oxford: Oxford University Press.

Lukács, G. [1938] 1980. "Realism in the Balance". See Adorno *et al.* (1980), 28–59.

Marx, K. [1859] 1994. "Preface to *A Contribution to the Critique of Political Economy*". In *Karl Marx: Selected Writings*, L. H. Simon (ed.), 209–13. Indianapolis, IN: Hackett.

Matisse, H. [1908] 1993. "Notes of a Painter". See Harrison & Wood (1993), 72–8.

McEvilley, T. 2010. *Yves the Provocateur: Yves Klein and Twentieth-Century Art*. Kingston, NY: McPherson.

Mothersill, M. 1986. *Beauty Restored*. Oxford: Clarendon Press.

Murdoch, I. 1985. *The Sovereignty of Good*. London: Ark.

Nead, L. 1992. *The Female Nude: Art, Obscenity and Sexuality*. London: Routledge.

Newman, B. 1993. "Interview with Dorothy Gees Seckler". See Harrison & Wood (1993), 764–66. [Originally published in *Art in America* (Summer 1962), 87.]

Nussbaum, M. C. 1990a. *Love's Knowledge: Essays on Philosophy and Literature*. Oxford: Oxford University Press.

Nussbaum, M. C. 1990b. "Flawed Crystals: James's *The Golden Bowl* and Literature as Moral Philosophy". See Nussbaum (1990a), 125–47. [Originally published in *New Literary History* **15**(1) (1983), 25–50.]

Nussbaum, M. C. 1990c. "'Finely Aware and Richly Responsible': Literature and the Moral Imagination". See Nussbaum (1990a), 148–67. [Originally published as "'Finely Aware and Richly Responsible': Moral Attention and the Moral Task of Literature", *Journal of Philosophy* **82**(10) (1985), 516–29.]

Peirce, C. S. 1940. *The Philosophy of Peirce: Selected Writings*. London: Routledge & Kegan Paul.

Plato 1963. *The Republic*. In *Plato: The Collected Dialogues*, E. Hamilton & H. Cairns (eds), 575–844. Princeton, NJ: Princeton University Press.

Richter, G. 1995. *The Daily Practice of Painting: Writings 1962–1993*. London: Thames & Hudson.

Savile, A. 1982. *The Test of Time: An Essay in Philosophical Aesthetics*. Oxford: Clarendon Press.

Scruton, R. 1997. *The Aesthetics of Music*. Oxford: Oxford University Press.

Scruton, R. 2009. *Beauty*. Oxford: Oxford University Press.

Segal, H. 2004. "A Psycho-Analytical Approach to Aesthetics". In *Psychoanalysis and Art*, S. Gosso (ed.), 42–61. London: Karnac. [Originally published in *International Journal of Psycho-Analysis* **33** (1952), 196–207.]

Sibley, F. 2001. "Why the *Mona Lisa* May Not be a Painting". In his *Approach to Aesthetics: Collected Papers on Philosophical Aesthetics*, J. Benson, B. Redfern & J. Roxbee-Cox (eds), 256–72. Oxford: Clarendon Press.

Stecker, R. 1997. *Artworks: Definition, Meaning, Value*. University Park, PA: Pennsylvania State University Press.

Stolnitz, J. 1992. "On the Cognitive Triviality of Art". *British Journal of Aesthetics* **32**(3): 191–200.

Sylvester, D. 1996. *About Modern Art: Critical Essays 1948–1996*. London: Chatto & Windus.

Tanner, M. 1976. "Sentimentality". In *Art and Morality*, J. L. Bermudez & S. Gardner (eds), 95–110. London: Routledge.

Tate 2008. "Press Release: Tate Acquires Louise Bourgeois Giant Spider, *Maman*" (14 January). www.tate.org.uk/about/press-office/press-releases/tate-acquires-louise-bourgeoiss-giant-spider-maman (accessed August 2012).

Tolhurst, W. 1979. "On What a Text Is and How It Means". *British Journal of Aesthetics* **19**(1): 3–14.

Vermazen, B. 1986. "Expression as Expression". *Pacific Philosophical Quarterly* **67**: 196–234.

Walton, K. 1977. "Review of Dickie's *Art and the Aesthetic*". *Philosophical Review* **86**(1): 97–101.

Walton, K. 1987. "Categories of Art". In *Philosophy Looks at the Arts*, J. Margolis (ed.), 53–79. Philadelphia, PA: Temple University Press. [Originally published in *Philosophical Review* **79**(3) (1970), 334–67.]

Walton, K. 1990. *Mimesis as Make-Believe*. Cambridge, MA: Harvard University Press.

Walton, K. 2006. "On the (So-called) Puzzle of Imaginative Resistance". In *The Architecture of the Imagination: New Essays on Pretence, Possibility, and Fiction*, S. Nichols (ed.), 137–48. Oxford: Oxford University Press.

Walton, K. 2008. "Transparent Pictures: On the Nature of Photographic Realism". In his *Marvellous Images: On Values and the Arts*, 79–116. Oxford: Oxford University Press. [Originally published in *Noûs* 18(1) (1984), 67–72.]

Williams, B. 1985. *Ethics and the Limits of Philosophy*. London: Fontana.

Wimsatt, W. K. & M. C. Beardsley 1976. "The Intentional Fallacy". In *On Literary Intention: Critical Essays*, D. Newton-de Molina (ed.), 1–13. Edinburgh: Edinburgh University Press. [Originally published in W. K. Wimsatt, *The Verbal Icon: Studies in the Meaning of Poetry* (Lexington, KY: University of Kentucky Press, 1954), 3–18.]

Wollheim, R. 1973a. "Minimal Art". In his *On Art and the Mind: Essays and Lectures*, 101–11. London: Allen Lane. [Originally published in *Arts Magazine* (January 1965): 26–32.]

Wollheim, R. 1973b. "The Work of Art as Object". In his *On Art and the Mind: Essays and Lectures*, 112–29. London: Allen Lane. [Originally published in *Studio International* (December 1970) **180**(928), 231–5.]

Wollheim, R. 1980. "Seeing As, Seeing In, and Pictorial Representation". In his *Art and Its Objects*, 205–26. Cambridge: Cambridge University Press.

Wollheim, R. 1986. *The Thread of Life*. Cambridge: Cambridge University Press.

Wollheim, R. 1987. *Painting as an Art*. London: Thames & Hudson.

Wollheim, R. 1994a. "The Sheep and the Ceremony". In his *The Mind and Its Depths*, 1–21. Cambridge, MA: Harvard University Press. [Leslie Stephen Lecture, originally published as *The Sheep and the Ceremony* (Cambridge: Cambridge University Press, 1979).]

Wollheim, R. 1994b. "Pictorial Style: Two Views". In his *The Mind and Its Depths*, 171–84. Cambridge, MA: Harvard University Press. [Originally published in *The Concept of Style*, B. Lang (ed.), 129–45 (Philadelphia, PA: University of Pennsylvania Press, 1979).]

Wollheim, R. 2001. "On Pictorial Representation". In *Richard Wollheim on the Art of Painting*, R. van Gerwen (ed.), 15–27. Cambridge: Cambridge University Press. [Originally published in *Journal of Aesthetics and Art Criticism* **56** (1998), 217–26.]

Woolf, V. 1924. "Character in Fiction". *The Criterion* **2**(8): 409–30.

Wynne, F. 2007. *I was Vermeer: The Forger who Swindled the Nazis*. London: Bloomsbury.

INDEX